First English Edition - December 2021

Foreword

The author left this letter with the manuscript:

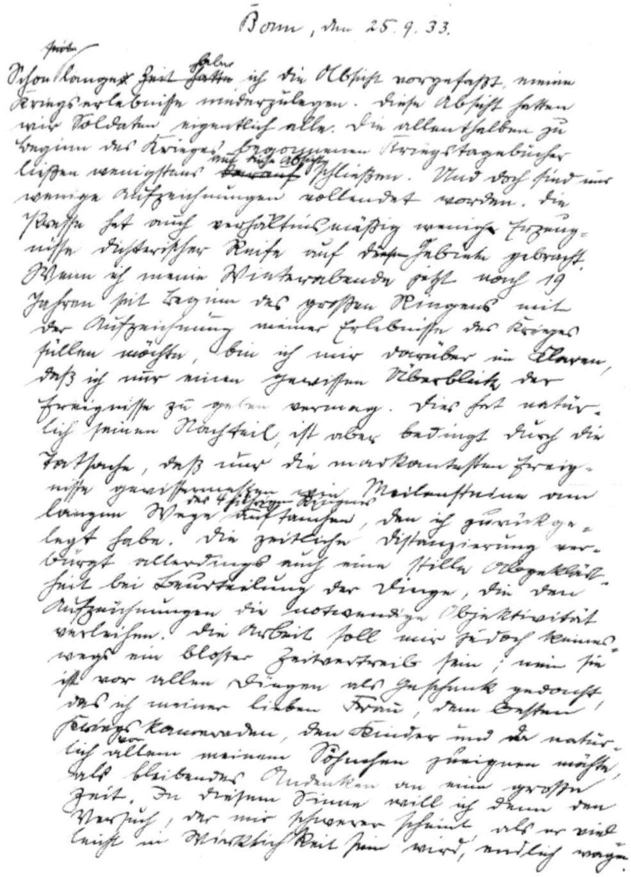

Bonn, den 25.9.33.

Schon lange habe ich die Absicht vorgefasst, meine Kriegserlebnisse niederzulegen. Diese Absicht hatten wir Soldaten eigentlich alle. Die allenthalben zu Beginn des Krieges begonnenen Kriegstagebücher ließen wenigstens auf diese Absicht schließen. Und doch sind nur wenige Aufzeichnungen vollendet worden. Die Presse hat auch verhältnismäßig wenige Erzeugnisse literarischer Kunst auf diesem Gebiete gebracht. Wenn ich meine Winterabende jetzt nach 19 Jahren seit Beginn des großen Ringens mit der Aufzeichnung meiner Erlebnisse des Krieges füllen möchte, bin ich mir darüber im Klaren, daß ich nur einen gewissen Überblick der Ereignisse zu geben vermag. Das hat natürlich seinen Nachteil, ist aber bedingt durch die Tatsache, daß nur die markantesten Ereignisse wie Meilensteine am langen Wege der 4jährigen Kriegszeit auftauchen, den ich zurückgelegt habe. Die zeitliche Distanzierung verbürgt allerdings auch eine stille Abgeklärtheit bei Beurteilung der Dinge, die den Aufzeichnungen die notwendige Objektivität verleihen. Die Arbeit soll mir jedoch keineswegs ein bloßer Zeitvertreib sein; mir ist sie vor allen Dingen als Geschenk gedacht, das ich meiner lieben Frau, den besten Kriegskameraden, den Kindern und natürlich allen meinen Schwestern zueignen möchte, als bleibendes Andenken an eine große Zeit. In diesem Sinne will ich denn den Versuch, der mir schwerer scheint als er vielleicht in Wirklichkeit sein wird, endlich wagen.

Bonn, 25.9.33

For some time now, I have had the intention of writing down my war experiences. Actually, all of us soldiers had this intention. The war diaries that were started everywhere at the beginning of the war at least suggested this intention. And yet only a few records were completed. The press has also produced relatively few products of poetic maturity in this field. If I want to fill my winter evenings now, after 19 years since the beginning of the great struggle, with a record of my experiences of the war, I am aware that I can only give a certain overview of the events. This has its disadvantages, of course, but is conditioned by the fact that only the most striking events appear, as it were, like milestones on the long road of the 4-year struggle that I have covered. The temporal distance, however, also guarantees a quiet detachment in the assessment of things, which gives the records the necessary objectivity. The work is by no means meant to be a mere pastime for me; no, it is intended above all as a gift that I would like to give to my dear wife, as my best war comrade, to the children and of course above all to my little son, as a lasting souvenir of a great time. With this in mind, I finally want to make the attempt.

Editor's Note

We, as the immediate family of Wimar Schmitz, received the manuscript from his daughter Anneli Jarm (née Schmitz) many years ago. This consists of about 180 typewritten pages.

We have captured the manuscript word for word. We have, in the German Edition as published in late 2020, left the grammar as in the original manuscript. It reflects, according to us, the way of speaking at the time the manuscript was written. In this English edition, we have also sought to keep the flavour of the grammar, although some of it may have become lost in the translation.

We hope it gives the reader an insight into the thinking at the time of the First World War; the motivations of the soldier, his fears and his hopes. The reader must have an understanding for the context of certain expressions and world views - these are the signs of the time of the First World War and the years after.

Dirk Els

December 2021, Johannesburg, South Africa

Table of Contents

List of Illustrations

PART 1: WAR!

1. War Volunteer

Illustration 1: Wimar Peter Schmitz

Inferiority. Something I was not indifferent to.

The wind had long since blown the evil leaves away when we set off for the nearby Rhine town of Neuwied.

We could not get into the usual good mood. Even the encounter with our old acquaintances from the most beautiful Rhine journey we ever made, did not blur the shadows that had crossed our path and whose distant reality was fire and blood.

This memorable Sunday was followed by a week so rich in fateful events that we had never seen before in our lives. Political intrigue and perfidy brought mobilisation and war on Friday. This fact seemed inconceivable to us, and yet the iron had been forged against Germany. More and more wolves found themselves ready to pounce on us.

I was seized by an inordinate anger, and it was immediately clear that I would not stand idly by.

Should I enlist as a war volunteer?

I did not find much support for this intention, neither from my relatives nor from my friends. The father who could have advised me had been snatched away from me by death many years ago. I had already got used to making my own decisions.

With my brother, a seminarian, I agreed to join the army. Without further ado, I resigned from my service and moved to the infantry barracks on Ermekeilstraße. But lo and behold, this was blocked. There were too many people there who thought like me and no provision had been made for such an influx. It was not until the afternoon of 4 August 1914 that I had the opportunity to state my intention and to present myself for a medical examination. I was weighed and this time found not "too light". Now I was one of the thousands upon thousands who stood ready with heart and hand. It was hard to keep order in the unruly tangle of new soldiers. This finally succeeded to a modest extent when we were broken up into smaller squads, so-called corporal groupings, and had received a commander.

And what commanders we had! Bourgeois fathers from Bonn, members of the Landsturm, took us under their wing.

Now, however, the new-born soldiery also wanted to be accommodated. That was also made possible. There were dance halls in Bonn and there was also straw. What more belongs to a soldier's emergency accommodation?

Late at night, I too found myself in the straw in a Poppelsdorf farm hall. With a quickly learned soldier's song on our lips, we went to the Ermekeil barracks every morning to receive our essential basic training. This had already begun when we were still in civilian clothes. You just have to imagine such a crowd. One of us in a blue suit with a straw hat, the other in this outfit, and the other probably still in knee breeches.

But soon also there was the Kaiser's skirt. It was a little worn and battered, but it did its job.

Now we were even let loose on humanity and allowed to be seen in uniform in the city.

What we lacked in soldierly requirements during the day, we made up for in the evening, drinking beer with our brave corporals. It was a great time of training, we with our good will to perform and our superiors with good insight and much forbearance. Truly a good unison. And what did we not experience on our marches and combat exercises in the beautiful surroundings of our Bonn garrison.

The enthusiasm that met us war volunteers everywhere is unimaginable today.

Although I had many acquaintances among my comrades, I got to know a Pomeranian who shared quarters with me. Now that our battalion had moved out, the mass accommodation was followed by the much more pleasant private quarters. This Pommer, a strapping blond boy, a merchant by trade, was a brilliant soldier. Unfortunately, we were soon separated, because he joined the teams that later formed the Reserve Infantry Regiment 236 and I remained with the Bonn garrison.

My military training was abruptly interrupted in the fourth week by a small writer's war. It happened like this: One of my colleagues, a former sergeant, like many who had found a job in the town hall, had been drafted and was competing with a younger sergeant for the sergeant's business at the recruit depot. They had no real use for him and had him take up the muster roll for the young recruits. This man had been ordered to bring to Magdeburg French and Belgian officers who had been wounded and taken prisoner, but who had in the meantime become fit for camp.

They were now looking for another muster roll collator and since I had met my colleague in the barracks yard, he drew attention to me and suggested me as his successor. At the evening parole, everyone called Schmitz had to come forward, and 18 representatives of the Rhenish noble family of the von Schmitzens came forward and I was quickly found to be the one who knew how to write, without actually knowing what was intended for me.

When I reported to the writing room, I was asked if I could write a muster roll. Although I did not know this important writing work, I promptly answered "Yes," because I said to myself, others before you have also been able to do it. And it also turned out afterwards that I was up to the unappealing office performance.

If, however, I had regarded this activity as a temporary "pressure point" which I welcomed with consideration for my worn through feet, I was disappointed after only a week to find that the intention was to make a regular hack out of me. Making contact with the omnipotent sergeant, made it possible for me to make my rejection of this known immediately and to demand categorically that I be placed in the "field serviceable company" that had been formed in the meantime. My comrades had already joined it. I succeeded in doing so after another week.

My comrades, however, were already well ahead of me in the hurried training. Now it was time to catch up. What a difference, the weeks that followed, filled with combat exercises and marches in wartime equipment, and the past weeks in the dull writing room. Above all, the night exercises, which took us to Rohleber, Holzlar and Niederpleis and always cost a lot of blanks, were wonderful.

For the time being, we considered the sandbags in the knapsacks to be unnecessary ballast. Therefore, the people behind had to remove them from the "monkeys on our backs" and empty them onto the Rhine bridge. Then we could find our way back, we told ourselves. What thoughts might the bridge staff have had on the following day about this sprinkling, which was actually only intended for icy conditions.

An unforgettable day's march led us through the Siebengebirge with a battle-like development towards Honnef. Were the inhabitants of the village and town enthusiastic! The Hotel Margaretenhof brought us a few buckets of milk and a lot of white bread to the march road. The head of the company marching into Honnef was bombarded with filled wine bottles. The bulk of the company, which had come up in the meantime, received cigars and cigarettes by the case from the hotel guests on the ferry in Königswinter.

With all this activity, our actually still quite tender bones did not notice too much of the strain of the march and the hellishly heavy luggage.

The shooting exercises on the Venusberg were of a more serious nature, but the results, as we were grumblingly told, were quite poor.

In the meantime, there were already wounded officers in our company who, although not yet completely healed, were teaching us the warlike polish and placed less emphasis on the drill. They were splendid fellows for whom we gladly went through thick and thin.

Illustration 2: New Soldiers

2. To the Front

On 22 October 1914, following the call for replacements, we were thought to have been shaken into shape for our departure to the front. We received our long-awaited field-grey uniform and the brand-new equipment. We also bought binoculars, a torch, a dagger knife and a war diary that was never written in. One last home holiday, another visit from my loved ones at the garrison and off we went, early in the morning of 24 October 1914, with jingling music and lots of flowers to the Bonn train station, where we were loaded onto a passenger train.

There were many Bonn boys among us, which is why our departure was particularly lively and tearful. I hadn't told my family the time of departure because I didn't like the maudlin farewell scenes.

Finally, we left, covered in flowers, in the direction of Godesberg, not really feeling what such a journey could mean. In Mehlem we were already fed. But only a few of us had rice soup with beef put into our new cooking utensils. We had had too much of a good thing first in Bonn. Our journey then continued through the romantic Ahr valley to Gerolstein. I didn't get the impression that they were in a hurry to get us to the front. Gerolstein was only reached in the evening darkness. Here, too, there was a stop. The other trains seemed to be in a much greater hurry than we were. The stay at the stations was always filled with all kinds of mischief. We had a particularly good time in Gerolstein. There were a lot of stacked up fruit baskets, waiting to be transported. There were also filled beer barrels. Assuming the consent of the owners, we brought a good deal of these supplies onto the train.

The following night's journey from Trier to Metz to Diedenhofen was filled with beer. It was difficult to serve the beer because we had no barrel taps. Much of the noble liquid was lost and did not promote the already existing "thick air" in the wagons.

In Diedenhofen we said goodbye to Germany. A circle of young girls - Red Cross volunteers - sang us the beautiful song: "übers Jahr, mein Schatz, übers Jahr" as we departed. These lovely melodies echoed in our ears as we passed the French border at Veuch.

We reached the town of Longwy at dawn. I had positioned myself in a brake house for better observation. A cold, damp mist crept over the ruins of the town. In this brake house, I had the undisturbed opportunity to let the impressions of the landscape take effect on me. The destruction looming in front of me depressed me a little and I involuntarily started thinking about the fighting that must have taken place here; then I saw German field-greys stumbling around among the ruins. They were getting their morning coffee from a steaming field kitchen. Otherwise, it was quiet in this town, as if it had died out. The day remained cold and hazy. Only here and there did the rising morning wind push the wisps of fog apart and allow a further glimpse into the undulating terrain.

The change in the settlements compared to the German villages of the day before was unmistakable. The buildings made a less well-kept, somewhat gloomy impression. This may also have been due to the sparse lighting.

I didn't lose this impression even when manor houses, hidden in gardens, occasionally appeared.

Here and there I saw prisoner squads working along the railway embankment. The civilian population, which was not very visible, was understandably quite unfriendly. They turned their backs - the second face - to the train. Particularly angry representatives even made signs that were supposed to mean cutting off of necks. These gestures were acknowledged by the travelling troops with guffaws.

The usual singing and noise in the train became more and more sparse. There was too much to see and say to each other. At Sedan, I finally got down from my post because I was expecting to stay in this town. And that was exactly what happened.

A large barrack accommodated us here not far from the station and we were given a rich and tasty meal. The length of our stay could not be determined with the best will in the world. However, the city interested us so much that we went "at ease" on an information trip. We took the rifles - our brides - with us.

Sedan itself showed no significant traces of the war. We found an opportunity here to send greetings to our homeland and helped ourselves to the postcards for sale. There was also wine to drink here. The smaller inns were called "Estaminet". Pale girls served us in silence and remained silent even when we tried to speak our meagre French. When we had also paid a visit to the beautification service[1], we were urged to march back and were just in time to catch our transport train.

Of course, our outing earned us a deafening bawl.

The afternoon, with friendly weather and the enjoyment of red wine, brought more movement into the troupe. At every station there was an opportunity to buy wine. Women and children crowded up to the wagons and lively sought buyers for their goods. The wine was thin and bad. In any case, the prices were in inverse proportion to the advertised goods. Nevertheless, people bought. We all still had money.

The journey to Charlerange in the Champagne region took the whole afternoon. Here the proximity to the front was already noticeable. The thunder of guns mingled with the usual din of a station teeming with troops and

---

[1] Verschönerungsrat = literally "beautifying council": common term in the war: for example hair barbers.

wounded transports. Only at a late hour did it seem possible to prepare a brew for us in heavy kettles over an open wood fire.

The flickering fire illuminated the warlike figures like a ghost. But suddenly a kettle with the hot broth broke off and the entire contents poured hissing over the burning logs, ran eagerly after the splitting crowd and scalded a few soldiers' paws.

So, it was nothing with a warm drink and we ducked back into our wagons. No sooner had we worked out where to sleep on the onward journey than we were told: "all get out".

We were in Sommepy. The proximity of the front forbade the use of light of any kind and we soon found ourselves in the peasant darkness of the village.

Chattering, we now stood and lay next to our rifle pyramids.

The front was silhouetted against the night sky by the flares that lit up everywhere, running irregularly in front of us. Some of these trembling lights burned so long and glided, slow falling, in the night sky. These were, we later realised, the French, silk parachuted, flares. Apparently, no accommodation was provided. We could go and find accommodation as we saw fit.

I, with many comrades, found my way to the church. Horses had stood here, then even the wounded had been accommodated there, and finally the church served as emergency quarters.

Straw was available and soon our tired bones were lying on the damp, cold scree.

However, the muddy night wind, which penetrated the large holes that shells had broken into the wall, soon woke even the most tired soldiers' bodies. Soon there was a fire burning in the church. The smoke from the wet fuel did not penetrate straight through the many holes in the roof. No, it crept over the carbolic-smelling storage areas and made it impossible to stay.

A change of quarters, in the otherwise completely shot-up district, brought no significant relief, and, as the first streaks of dusk became visible on the horizon, we went in search of a field kitchen. We soon found it, for they give themselves away by their inviting smells. The kitchen belonged to the cuirassiers, but we got something to eat and warmed our frozen hands with the hot cups. We couldn't drink from the cups yet, but the feeling of having the pleasure in sight made us happy beyond measure.

The fire-making in the church must have been extended somewhat afterwards; they must not have been particularly careful in the choice of fuel either, for the cavalry created a terrible row afterwards.

As the daylight grew, we took a closer look at the scene and found that quite nice quarters could have been made up in parts of the town across the Py stream.

At about 10 o'clock in the morning we arrived in the meadow in front of the village and after standing for a long time we were greeted very warmly by our regimental commander and distributed to the individual companies.

We were even allowed to express wishes regarding the allocation, which were taken into account as far as possible.

I left my allocation to chance and joined the 8th Company.

The regiment was in position, and we were given a short grace period. It must not have been the reputation of being able soldiers that preceded us, because we experienced 8 days of informative drill in the neighbouring village of St. Marie a Py.

This village, situated on an undulating, woodless hill and crossed by the Py stream, became the regiment's second home for months. Our quarters were the cellars of the shot-up houses, as well as low shelters around the village cemetery. These shelters had the advantage over the vaulted cellars that they were not so rat-infested.

We also felt quite comfortable here. I lived in such an earth dwelling with 8 comrades.

Our training at St. Marie a Py consisted mainly of combat shooting. No great precautions were taken against accidents or injuries to bystanders. Figures were set up in the manner of recumbent shooters and the banging went off merrily. Since the shooting usually took place in groups, the so-called bad shooters could not be identified. This also meant that there was no additional drill for such unlucky shooters. The routes to and from the shooting range were designed as a field exercise.

The unadorned hill, devoid of any lush vegetation, was crowned by a large statue of the Virgin Mary surrounded by a few living trees. Otherwise, there was not a single tree or shrub on this stony height. From here, one could see far into the rolling countryside of the Ardennes, a circumstance that may have led to a battery being dug in here during the advance. The traces of the command posts were still clearly visible. But the impact was also visible in the many deep shell holes in the chalky rocky soil.

Strangely enough, the figure of Our Lady did not show the slightest trace of damage.

Our platoon leader, a deputy officer from the crafts in Koblenz, never failed to stop us for a short prayer at the statue, reciting prayers himself. A bullet to the head made it a painless end for him during the violent reconnaissance on Christmas Eve 1914. A pity about this excellent leader.

We spent the cool evenings of this short week camped by the smouldering embers of burnt-out fires. Old familiar songs of the soldiers and the homeland blared through the night, blending strangely with the fading sound of the front.

A strange smell crept from the ruins of the village. Decomposing and charred animal carcasses under the rubble of the ruins and stinging smoke of resinous pine rising from hidden field kitchens combined to create what could truly be called the air of war.

And yet I would have missed something in this landscape and mood if it hadn't been for this doom-laden air around my nose.

In the course of the post-war years, I have seen many a more or less lifelike war film. Again and again, I thought, well, that's a deceptive imitation, only the air, the real atmosphere of war, is missing.

As is well known, there is no such thing as a soldier's camp without guards. That's why camp and field guards were also issued here.

In the two hours of nocturnal, solitary wandering around the cemetery, there was so much opportunity to indulge one's thoughts. With a little bit of imagination, pale skulls could be seen from the small, battered white grave crosses of the cemetery, sparsely illuminated by the moon. All sorts of creepy things could be put together on them. Then there was the distant clatter of the front and the sparse fireworks of the flares.

A good overture to the real drama that we were soon to get to know.

3. Into the Fire

One day, the company sergeant with his scribe came to us from the position - that's what we called the trench - to prepare the newcomers for the upcoming unification with the front company. One fine afternoon, the all-powerful company mother stands before the enlisted replacement section. Short and stocky, with a full beard, he stands there, the little man. His field-grey suit resembled a miller's robe, so full of chalk dust was he. His boots were also white. He looked at us as real sergeants are able to. Everything is caught up in one glance, what is good and what is bad.

He will probably have liked our enthusiastic looks best of all.

He described the conditions at the front, gave an overview of what Field Company 8/160 had already achieved, and deeply regretted the many losses that urgently required replacements.

We heard from him that our company was not directly in the trench but had to cover the artillery. In two days, however, we were to go into the front trench together. We also received instructions on how to behave on this occasion and were eagerly awaiting the things that were now to follow on our contemplative Landsknecht life here in the village.

The last day in the village was reserved for a particularly thorough cleaning of our weapons and finally led us together once again to the village church, which had been badly damaged by the war, where we held a small devotion. These devotions, which also followed later, did not in any way emphasise any particular religion and that seemed to me to be so unifying and comradely.

Before nightfall, we set out on our first memorable march to our fighting unit. Strange thoughts may well have arisen in all of us on the silent march through the undulating landscape dotted with many small pine groves, and a silent last communion may have been held with home and loved ones.

Panting and dripping with sweat, we reached the field artillery command posts loaded with our heavy baggage after about 1½ hours of marching and settled into the light dugouts driven into embankments that our company held.

We had not received any bombardment up to this point and thought that our sergeant's descriptions of the front were somewhat exaggerated.

Quickly stowed away in the shelters, we very soon fell asleep.

In the morning we got to know our company. They were all white limestone figures with beards and shaggy hair. Now we were divided into platoons and groups.

The existing material of old fighters was loosened up and the composition of the groups (8 men strong) was usually like this: 2 active, 2 reservists, 2 soldiers and 2 war volunteers.

This mixture was good.

In all likelihood, this was the best way for us to get into shape.

My group was led by a non-commissioned officer, the length of a tree, who went by the beautiful name of Herring. He was a merchant who had served for a year and was very fond of alcoholic beverages, but a very concerned, loyal-hearted fellow. The two active men were middle class Rhenish farmers. One of the two reservists was a musician. He was playing first violin in a café when the war took him by surprise. The other reservist was a watchmaker in his father's shop. The Landwehr men, dressed in black coats (we had the other field grey right away), were staid fellows from the Krefeld area. Helenenbrunn was their hometown. They had such dignified beards, one dark and pointed, the other so beautifully rounded by his shaggy full beard. Both of us volunteers must have identified ourselves, with our milk-faced faces, as nice nosy greenhorns.

We did not have an easy time of it, placed in this circle. Most of the camp functions fell to us, who were called co-volunteers. We liked it quite well in the gnarled pine grove.

Although the "old men" had no pronounced preference for being fired upon by enemy artillery, they did long for a little “cannoning” for our sake, in order to find out whether we were as brave and courageous, as we seemed to be cheeky and good-for-nothing. This wish came true around noon, and somewhat abundantly. Yes, I must say, at first it seemed a bit grumpy to me how the iron portions came howling along and then died with a heavy bang. But the scare didn't last long, and because the shelters, squeezed into steep embankments, were spared, we quickly recovered from the initial shock. Nevertheless, the impression these little things could make on us in the open was a bitter foretaste, but for the time being we were not yet in the open. There had been those who now told the most horrible things about the advance, which they had gone through with all its horrors, but also with all its romance.

So this day also passed without any particular difficulties and the evening darkness was now to be our protector on our way into the trench to relieve the tired, lame comrades so that they could stretch properly again after 4 days of underground life.

When we set off, we were told to be extremely quiet, not to turn on any lights, to keep our torches in our pockets, our drinking cups in our haversacks, to be united in our approach, to stay awake at all times and to keep in touch.

Now the journey began. Through scrub and battered forest plots, whose tree population was already very taken along. Numerous white shell holes grinned at us. Then we went again partly through poor trenches, then again over fallow fields. All of a sudden, when we were standing nicely on a "presentation plate", we were under fire. Most of the fire was shrapnel, which was unloaded on us. We splattered apart and lay on the ground in a flash, slipping into shell holes and ducking against their walls. It all happened in a fraction of a second.

Then I heard cries of pain. Some of us had been hit.

Shrapnel wounds were particularly feared. Those filthy, misshapen, crushed lumps of lead. When there was a minute's lull in the firing, we were on our feet again and rushing forward. Emotionally, we were catching up again to some extent. Then I suddenly slipped into a ditch. Of course, I couldn't see anything clearly in the darkness, so I slowly felt my way along. Suddenly I saw a very faint glimmer of light in front of me. I soon crawled up and, pushing aside a canvas, landed in a hole in the ground inhabited by telephone operators from the artillery observation. Glad to have found comrades, I was now informed how to proceed. Soon I knew the direction and approximate distance to the fighting trench, waited for the next greeting from the French and started for the trench as best I could in the pathless jumble of rubble and wire.

I reached it without any service injury.

I was by no means the last of the noble bunch. It was pitch dark in the trench, which was so wide that one could have driven through it with the field kitchen; but sometimes not, because the moon pushed its silver light out from between the wispy clouds and flares sometimes gave off their ghostly, restless light.

After many futile attempts, I was finally granted a place in a hole in the ground.

I didn't need to yet stand guard in the unknown trench.

In the meantime, the shooting had stopped in this section. The Frenchmen were peppering another area to worry the food fetchers and messengers on their nightly secret routes. The clapping of infantry shells as they hit in front of our trench, the singing of shells passing overhead and the slow hammering of French machine guns was the new night music that soon lulled me, tired young warrior, to sleep. The night had passed without an artillery concert.

Early in the morning I took a careful look at the whole operation. As far as I could determine, the ditch ran in an irregular course through lightly undulating terrain and became entangled in a former pine grove. I say former grove because I don't think I can address the crownless mostly splintered and bent groups of trees as a forest anymore. It resembled a large hedgehog rather than a forest. With a little caution, one also had the opportunity to eye the enemy's terrain. In front of me was a meadow with a small river running through it, the Suippe. The meadow terrain still showed traces of willow huddles. The easily recognisable French trench system was staggered one behind the other and connected with running trenches - as I was later instructed. To the left, on the side of a hill, were the ruins of a windmill; behind it, a few hundred metres further on, was the village of Souvain. Behind the stream, about 400 metres away from our trench, a farm that had not yet been completely razed to the ground, lay just in front of me in the middle of the tangle of trenches. Sandbag-protected trenches ran through the outbuildings.

Blue smoke rose straight up to the sky from this idyll.

Very light wisps of mist rolled through the valley.

Even the chirping of birds could be heard. A peaceful picture, I thought to myself, and this is how the infernal front is supposed to look?

I was quite satisfied. I expressed my satisfaction later to my corporal. He said: "I hope you stay satisfied for a long time.

But at 8 o'clock the iron portions of Schangel[2] came wobbling along and pelted down in the immediate vicinity of the trench. That resulted in chunks and smoke and stench and splinters and limestones whirring around our heads. None of the fat beans got into the trench. The shooting didn't last long either.

But the greetings were soon returned with Prussian economy by our artillery.

---

[2] French were called "Schangels", a slang expression for the French "Jean"

We had the opportunity to observe the hits and their effects through the open shields. Duds, which were very common with French shells, were almost non-existent.

Then it was quiet again for hours on both sides, apart from the rifle shots that went on all day.

We passed the time, as far as we were on duty, as trench guards, with all kinds of more or less important things, but unfortunately very little with food and drink. We only had food at night and a bottle of coffee or tea at the same time.

The lack of food could not be compensated for in any way in the trenches unless the knapsack contained some kind of supply, and this was seldom the case - apart from smoking material. On the other hand, when it rained, there was the possibility of quenching thirst, and this was done in the form of stretching out a more or less clean sheet of tent, with its gutter-like slope to a cooking pot or drinking cup. The inherently bad taste of the water was improved by adding a crushed peppermint biscuit.

The nature of the earth, which, as I said, consisted of chalk rocks, gave us the opportunity to practise a certain sculpting art. Under the hands of skilful comrades, the most beautiful souvenirs were created from this very soft stone material, which could be worked with a pocketknife. Some people also had the idea of making postcards out of birch bark with simple painting and appropriate lettering to indicate the current situation and entrusting them to the field post office for delivery. A noble competition soon befell all comrades in the practice of these peaceful activities in quiet hours and it was a nice balance to the rough and tumble of war. Many a German home may still be adorned with products from these strange art workshops in the trenches of Champagne as a reminder of a great time.

On the first evening in position, I had the opportunity to see for myself under what difficult circumstances the little food had to be brought in. I was appointed to fetch food for our group.

Armed with 4 cooking utensils and 9 canteens, I waited with my companions in a trench at nightfall for the signal to march off.

If I had expected a stimulating interruption from the trench monotony, I was soon sorely deceived. For we received the familiar firing raids that are inevitable even if the time for fetching food is set at a different time every evening. Complete silence cannot be achieved in such a food fetching caravan; not even if the cooking utensils were padded with cotton wool. That evening, we were also surprised by a cold rain that softened the ground and the trenches.

Finally, we arrived at the fragrant field kitchen in a small wood. The food is served in complete darkness and takes quite a while to fill the water bottles.

Now it's back over hill and dale and mud and mess. Always staying ahead and finally we are at the beginning of our running trench. The beautifully modelled stairway to its slippery bottom has become a slide and I have the misfortune to slip with 2 cooking utensils in each hand and the water bottles dangling around me. With the elegant arc my arms made on the involuntary journey, the cooking utensils did not remain at their lavish fullness. Not even the rain could make up for the loss, and my group made sour faces at the diminished portions and did not hold back with their "undisguised praise".

I affirmed my innocence of the painful loss. However, in this critical situation, my protestations lacked the necessary force. Something like this could only happen to someone who was willing to go to war. But it happened to other veteran warriors before me and after me, who had grown grey in gun smoke, and it will happen again in all coming trench wars.

That rainy night I had to stand my first listening post, a double shift from 2 - 4 am. My comrade-in-arms was the goateed Landwehrman from Helenenbrunn. For this significant service, one is woken up 10 minutes before time by trench guards. I didn't need to be woken up, because I wasn't asleep and was eagerly awaiting the things that were to come. And they came.

I climbed out of the trench with my partner, who was already familiar with the situation, by means of a birch ladder, and like him I struggled through the low tripwire enclosure and then under cheval-de-frise[3] into a shell hole that could have served as a bathtub, there was so much water in it.

The edge of the trench to the enemy's side made it possible to stay in the dry. I mean, what you could call dry that night. Here we lay down our guns, threw the safety catch off and sprang out into the night. Coloured scumbags were lying opposite us and grim reports were circulating about their sneakiness.

When a flare went up, you could see quite nicely what was going on in the foreground. Two hours of listening post duty can be a really long time. There were no incidents to report. The only lively thing that approached us was the shuttle patrol between the listening posts.

But it's nice when you come back from this duty and can then lie down in the shelter. And if you have a cigarette to go with it, then you feel blissful. For the uninitiated, it is difficult to imagine the cosy security that then takes possession of you in the low hole in the ground.

In the morning, the usual breakfast racket of the artillery on both sides begins. On this day we had our first casualty. It was a comrade from Siegburg, a seminarian. A large shrapnel, like a saw, had hit him in the neck. We new fighters were very moved, although this death did not

---

[3] Wooden frame defensive structure with barbed wire [German - Spanische Reiter – "spanish riders"]

really seem like a real, final death to us. I never lost that impression, even later when I saw many dead. The 4 days of trench duty were generally quite harmless compared to the events we experienced later at the same place. Then we were relieved, which meant we were allowed to return to our reserve village.

The four-day stay in the village after our first front experience was very pleasant. The market tender wagon that had just arrived, added to our sense of comfort with its beautiful, coveted sachets. The regimental band serenaded us every afternoon. We were able to walk around a lot after light duty and cook and boil so much that it had a style.

In the field of cooking, it turned out that I was not entirely untalented. Others had a special predisposition for procuring the cooking utensils, as we called all the things that needed and could be coughed up. What I never did was play cards, an activity that took up almost most of my comrades' free time.

In return, however, I wrote many letters and extended them to 8 or even more pages, which of course earned me a shake of the head from those less inclined to write. Since the so-called "third man" was always easy to find, I was also little pushed to play cards and so it happens that in my 5 years of war, military hospital, and captivity, I never touched a playing card.

Our third occupation of the trench was particularly remarkable. The march there in a hurry already cost us dead and wounded. The days themselves were also extremely warlike. The first attempted attack by our coloured opponents took place during this time. It was nipped in the bud, but for once it gave us the opportunity to take a closer look at these beasts and hear their roar. The French were themselves too clever to make the attempt and take a German trench that was in no way ready for assault. But for this, in a noble impulse, the drunken savages were just good enough for them. A failed attack, which, in addition costs the attackers considerable casualties, naturally causes particular anxiety in the front section. Artillery activity increases significantly. And one always has the feeling that what has been lost will soon be made up for. Efforts were also made; however, they were in vain due to the once aroused, increased attention of the troops.

So, this time the 4 days passed very varied and also brought us considerable losses from artillery. Unfortunately, after the relief we did not go to the village this time, but to the artillery cover, where we were very limited in our freedom of movement during the day. The enemy knew every path and footbridge here, every waterhole, and covered them heavily with shells and shrapnel.

Because life and activity here gave me little stimulation, I spent a lot of time with the artillerymen.

There were also two flat-bore guns of about 10 cm calibre that the Germans had captured from the French along with the ammunition. We called these guns the "senior teachers" because most of them were one-year-olds - philologists - in the operating crew. In recognition of my attachment to the artillery, one day I was allowed to fire a "senior instructor" while pulling on a rope. It so happened that my first shot against the enemy was not fired from a rifle of mine, as would have been expected as an infantryman, but from a French cannon.

But this was my only artillery action.

The increased unrest in our section of the front did not abate. It increased even more in the Perthes area and here the enemy, after having completely crushed the trench, succeeded in penetrating the front. A rifle battalion threw the enemy out of the trench again at dawn the following day without any artillery preparation.

Our battalion also belonged to the reserve thrown together for such purposes.

But since the guards made such a clean sweep, we remained only extras and had the opportunity to see how an unweakened active elite troop, which had not yet been worn down by any battle, knew how to die. Even the white French could not withstand this momentum in the least, and it can truly not be said that the French core troops were weak.

In the angry artillery fire of the enemy, we were soon able to retreat to our quarters with few losses. The mutual frontal events only increased in intensity. The resting position almost no longer deserved its beautiful name. The weather also became more and more unbearable. The streets in the village were covered with 10 cm of mud. Firewood was nowhere to be found. A medical water truck supplied us with boiling water. However, we could only get this if we could show a cooking utensil with soup cubes, coffee grounds or cocoa cubes.

4. First active combat action

In mid-December 1914, some wintry cold and light snowfall set in. This circumstance gave the airmen better observation of the field positions, trenches and approach routes and led to effective shooting, which we often had to feel bitterly. The lack of heating material and in many places also the impossibility of lighting fires because of the smoke development, made life even more difficult for us. Even plenty of warm clothes did not protect us completely, because they were mostly soaked and had to dry on our bodies.

In addition to the wounded, there were now more cases of acute colds, which thinned our ranks.

My group was still complete.

Christmas was approaching. Christmas in enemy territory. Who would have thought that in August, with the glorious, almost unbelievable successes of our troops? "We'll be in Paris in six weeks," the troops called to us in the first days of August.

And now we were busily preparing for a winter campaign.

According to our rotation, we were in artillery cover at Christmas. Our official communal Christmas party was therefore scheduled by the commander for 21 December.

The venue was St. Marie a Pz in a field barn that had been made up in a makeshift fashion.

There was a wonderfully moving celebration and afterwards much wine and grog. Of course, the gifts from our loved ones had not yet reached us so early. But a car of gifts of love, collected in Bonn for the Bonn II Battalion 160 arrived at the right time.

That evening I drank champagne for the first time in my humble life.

I still clearly remember the beautiful speech by our commander, Major Wagner, which ended with a cheer for our fatherland and reminded us of our loyalty to this country.

My gift package contained, among other things, a beautiful woollen blanket, fur-lined leather gloves, wrist warmers, stockings and a beautiful book. No one wore such beautiful gloves as I did. I later gave them to our little ensign "Püppchen[4]" who led the platoon. They served him better than they did me.

The following evening, we took up our artillery position.

Here, on 24 December, we were just about to make preparations for a small Christmas party in the dugouts, when in the afternoon our Major Wagner came to us with the news that the French had borrowed an advanced NCO post and occupied the position with machine guns. The

---

[4] little "Doll"

peace and order on Christmas Day required that the place be cleared up.

Fifty volunteers were wanted to carry out the operation. The old people, especially the fathers of families, should be spared.

Nearly 50 men volunteered from our company, which was about 160 strong.

Nevertheless, there were fathers of families among them.

We moved forward at nightfall with our assault packs, where we received our instructions.

A patrol wanted to know that the French had cleared the post. We therefore immediately took large spades with us, in order to properly develop the base, which was located in a forest top. Our advance also lacked the usual embarrassing caution and it seemed to be only a walk through the former forest. Suddenly, however, a frenzied shooters und M.G. fire spat at us and held an abundant harvest. A bloodcurdling roar penetrated the starry night. Everything took up position as best it could, that is, threw themselves down. There was a muddled confusion. Without waiting for the fire to subside, the command "Jump up, march, march" rang out, but not too many could follow. Then Sergeant Dung, who was leading the "violent reconnaissance", was shot in the head next to me.

A sergeant Hünten - today he is a police captain - snatched command and tried another jump. But the base was well occupied. The amount of rifle fire made it clear that our operation could not be carried out in this manner, and we were then also ordered to withdraw one by one, after reinforcements were not sent.

Dead and wounded had to be taken with us. Finally, we reached our initial position, but the wounded had not all returned. They were still screaming and moaning into the cold night.

We got them all in later because the French, expecting a new attack, had not followed us.

The leadership, recognising the difficult situation, did not want to make any further sacrifices and had decided with the artillery to bombard the foothold beforehand with shelling.

So, my first active combat action was visibly overshadowed by the unpleasantness of the circumstances.

I was disappointed and yet glad to have escaped with my skin intact.

The night was almost completely filled with the comradely activity of transporting the wounded to the dressing station, which I had to visit twice more.

Then I was done for and tried to find accommodation in one of the trench shelters, which I succeeded in doing after much pleading.

The rutted and hard-frozen ground had made our nightly transport work very difficult, for every bad step shook the wounded and caused considerable pain.

I therefore slept well into the morning and did not want to get out of my hole in the ground when the French poured more fire on our trench.

The last request from my comrades to come out and seek shelter behind the parapets I rebuffed with my reply that I had served as a target all night and had not been hit, and that as I was too tired, I would stay lying down. As I was lying all alone in the table-high hole in the ground and the impacts were coming closer and closer, I made up my mind to go to the trench to make use of all the possibilities of protection and, above all, to have contact with my comrades.

I had not yet crawled halfway out of the dugout when a big grenade hit directly behind my little dugout and thoroughly mixed everything up. My left arm dangled out out of the, God thank, light debris, The lime dirt in my mouth prevented the penetration of too much powder and sulphur vapour and I was soon pulled out by my comrades, badly damaged but still in good spirits.

In the company leader's dugout, I was given cognac and quickly recovered. The forehead above my right eye, still in the eyebrows, was torn. The left side of my chest was bleeding profusely. Both minor matters, as soon became apparent. The alarming flow of blood from my mouth soon stopped and seemed to have come from small local bruises.

By midday I had recovered to stay, but then heart trouble set in, and I was taken into custody until evening, when I was taken away.

In this way, the Christ Child gave me the journey home on Christmas Day.

5. Homewards

This was however connected with all kinds of circumstances and lasted more than 3 months.

At the dressing station, a rickety transport wagon - a horse-drawn cart - was waiting for me and several other wounded comrades, who limped with us to the battalion, where we arrived in the morning. From here we boarded the wounded transport train the next day.

Our journey ended in Vouziers. Here I was placed in the war hospital "Knabenschule[5]". This military hospital was only very poorly equipped with the most unbelievable beds. But we had it very good. I slept in a blue four-poster bed.

The very first night I had a strange experience. In a dream, I saw a hollow-cheeked face above me, wrapped in a robe, in a dimly lit sickroom in the middle of the night. The ghostly thin light made the motionless face appear to me as a bony face, and in my feverish delusion I must have regarded the apparition as a message of death. But my young body rebelled against it and with lightning speed I must have jumped out of bed. But that was reason enough for the 'good friar' - for that was what my nocturnal visitor was

---

[5] "Boys School"

- to flee the sickroom. A medical orderly who had been summoned calmed me down and, after I had been informed about the supposed ghost, I was also happy to calm down.

When the house had to be heavily occupied on another day, I was shunted on to Rethel.

Here I ended up in a factory hall. The transmissions on the ceiling undoubtedly marked the character of the room. The walls and ceilings were neatly painted white.

The number of wounded and sick people housed here, including mentally ill, seemed immense to me.

Here, too, a great effort was made to care for them. But it was not a place where one could approach recovery. Only the most necessary things could be done to ensure safe onward transport to the homeland.

The 3 days and nights I spent here were peppered with shattering events and horrors. There is no more beautiful death than being slain in front of the enemy, but there are wounds, as one could see here, that can instil the horror of war. In addition, there was that telling carbolic smell and the long restless hours of the night. I was very happy when I was called up for transport on the hospital train and allowed to leave this place again.

What looks I caught when I said goodbye!

I was comforted by the conviction that the suffering of these comrades was for the most part worse than one was inclined to assume in terms of danger to life. Most of them will probably have made the journey to Germany sooner or later after me.

Our hospital train to the homeland travelled very slowly compared to our longing, which was rushing by leaps and bounds.

In Diedenhofen I was still thinking about our farewell in October.

So, it hadn't turned out to be over a year, as the girls had sung.

Late in the evening, our train rattled across the beloved Rhine in Ludwigshafen and immediately afterwards we stopped in Mannheim. The question of where in Germany we should stay took up most of our interest. So, we immediately asked the train crew whether the journey was over or whether anything was known about the destination of the transport. So much could be ascertained that the intention was to separate the train here. One part was to remain in Mannheim and the other was to continue to Heidelberg. If I could not come to my homeland, I would have liked to experience moving into the city of the Muses, Heidelberg. How pleased I was when I was assured that I was on the part of the train that was leaving for Heidelberg. But far from it. Immediately, something started moving that literally left me standing and figuratively made me lie down, and that was the train to Heidelberg.

In the meantime, the transport of the wounded to hospitals in the city of Mannheim had begun and I was also with the last part of the fighters who were carefully packed into tram cars.

The nightly tram ride through the city seemed like an endless long journey. But even this journey came to an end, namely in front of a factory.

Oh dear, I thought to myself, now we're going to a factory again. Yes, it really was a factory, but we went into the feudal administration building of a rubber and celluloid factory.

It was 2 o'clock in the morning when I was bathed and brought to my room in tip-top shape.

A beautiful bright room with dazzling white beds awaited me here.

When I awoke from my death-like sleep at about 10 o'clock, I saw a young nurse standing over me. She looked at me seriously, but this time I did not immediately jump out of bed as if stung by a tarantula, as I had done in Vouziers.

The medical examination that soon followed was satisfactory. Unfortunately, the satisfactory condition did not last long.

My mother, who had been informed of my arrival at the military hospital, immediately visited me with my sister. My mother had never made a journey beyond Cologne and Koblenz in her life. But like so many mothers, she learned to travel during the war. After all, we were five boys in the field at the same time.

My rapidly deteriorating condition made it impossible to visit me for any length of time. I was only able to exchange a few words with my relatives. With heavy hearts, they returned home the following day with the indispensable intention of bringing me home in case I died. I lay in a fever for 14 days, which rose above 40 degrees.

But there was nothing to do with the expected death. After 3 months I made the journey home healthy and cheerful as never before. In 3 weeks, I had already improved so much that I was able to enjoy the real pleasure of being in hospital. But even surrounded by death, the soldier's life is also in the homeland, even under medical care.

I was to experience that too.

When I was able to leave the bed, I was longing for a warm bath. That was prepared for me at my request. But I almost drowned in it. It happened as follows: After my companion had brought me to the bathing cell, I closed the door and crawled into the hot water. Soon an oppressive feeling in my heart area came over me and I preferred to leave the broth as quickly as possible, so I fainted while squatting on the edge of the bathtub. Fortunately, I fell back onto the rubber carpet and not into the water. The supervisor, noticing my long absence, suddenly felt her heart bubbling and a search was made for me. The bathroom was locked and there was no answer to the repeated call. Therefore, door broken open and the Schmitz was found lying on the ground like a lump of misery.

This intermezzo brought me another week of careful nursing.

But I soon recovered properly and was allowed to tour the city.

I had to endure a full 3 months in Mannheim and it even took my gentle insistence for the very concerned, good chief doctor to discharge me.

What a reunion in my homeland!

The joy soon melted away, however, because I had to report to the garrison immediately. This I did after a few days.

In the spring of 1915, anyone who had come from a military hospital and was accepted into a wounded company in the garrison, which already strongly resembled the formal military strictness that had meanwhile emerged at home, felt this change quite palpably.

This is what happened to me when I arrived at the Bonn garrison.

I did not dare to expect a long life in the wounded company, because I thought I was healed and strengthened. But the strict staff doctor dictated that I should be fit for garrison duty for another two months.

6. Sideway Jumps

My effervescent courage to face life brought me two more trips to the Belgian front during this time, one of which was so remarkable that it should be described here.

It was to bring "meat sparrows" for the stew to the fighting troops. Our meat sparrows, however, were still live cows and oxen that came from Friesland and which we were to take into custody in Cologne and accompany to Flanders.

Farmers' sons who knew the art of milking were considered suitable for this command, for it is said to be torture for the animals to stand in the milk, as the technical term goes. Strangely enough, the sergeant, who probably suspected that I had a thousand skills, enjoined me to these 20 agricultural enthusiastic soldiers.

Instead of our previous lockless muskets of the old type, we were given nice 98-gauge rifles and locked up in the barracks so as not to take a too extended, self-important city- and country holiday, which would have been apt to result in an unpunctual start to the precious cattle action.

A locked door was not an insurmountable obstacle to our escape into bourgeois life. We bid a fond farewell to our benefactors and patrons before setting off on our great journey, and in the morning, we stood in the barracks yard, ready to march.

We went to the material depot at the goods station, where we received our armour in the form of two zinc-plate horse buckets each. With this additional, little-seen equipment, we took a passenger train to Cologne to the slaughter and cattle yard.

We met the many questions from the civilians about our military aims with a meaningful look at our buckets and the frank confession that we wanted to bail out the sea, meaning the Channel, so that England could be better dealt with.

The betrayal of this military secret understandably aroused great enthusiasm among the people of Cologne.

Our "sparrows" had not yet arrived in Cologne. We therefore occupied the hall of the livestock exchange and eagerly studied the lively activity of the many livestock commission agents and money changers. Our attention was also drawn to the hygienic facilities of the various types of animals in the slaughterhouse. The only thing that was really repulsive was the grim calm with which the Jewish avengers run their long knives down the animals' throats. I involuntarily drew comparisons with the fighting style of the

German soldiers and that of the Zuavs[6] in the front, who crawled with long knives in the filthy muzzle of the fore-terrain in order to flay us.

Even in the evening our animals had not yet arrived. This prompted me to make a trip into town on my own, where I stayed the night with acquaintances and said goodbye early in the morning with a fox - a 20-mark piece - and many wishes.

Around noon, the transport train with the livestock finally arrived. There were 500 head of cattle. A nice passenger coach was harnessed and the journey began. We stopped in Kalscheuren. A patrol through the village led so many milking maids to the train that the soldiers did not need to practise their half-learned milking skills. Milk was a much sought-after liquid, for which they were happy to use the patronage. At night we passed through Liège and then turned off towards the front in the French-Belgian corner in a very slow, often interrupted journey. I already knew Belgium from peacetime. In 1913, I had made a holiday trip to Ghent, Ostend and Bruges, so I was not particularly interested in the flat, uninviting landscape. In enemy territory there

---

[6] The Zouaves were a class of light infantry regiments of the French Army serving between 1830 and 1962 and linked to French North Africa, as well as some units of other countries modelled upon them. The zouaves, along with the indigenous Tirailleurs Algeriens, were among the most decorated units of the French Army. Wikipedia

were plenty of milkers and milkmaids who were happy to do the work for us.

Our first town was Roullers. Here we got rid of half of our cattle cars. We visited the town and went to the rendezvous. The rations money we had received were not used for this purpose. Soldiers' homes took care of our physical well-being.

The last of our cattle caravan was taken to a corps slaughterhouse near Zarren. There was still a paddock of about 50 head that we brought to this station. However, the slaughterhouse was not in the village of Zarren, but on its estate, about an hour away.

Some militia armed with truncheons had arrived in Zarren to receive the cattle. But it soon became apparent that the people had their work cut out for them to keep the caravan on the march. At the urgent request of the crews, some of us finally agreed to take part in the drive, in exchange for the promised excellent food on the estate.

Out of good humour, I also went along. The approaching darkness made our way very difficult. Again and again, the excited beasts strayed from the path and hopped into the ditches along the road, causing them to shy even more and wander haphazardly around the area. We finally arrived at the estate with only a small number of the animals. Attempts to keep an eye out for the stray animals by means of stable lanterns failed because the wind kept blowing out the lanterns.

The failure of the transport was, of course, on our account and so the promised rations were also correspondingly poor.

For sleeping accommodation, we were given a small chamber in which we laid fresh straw and soon we were sleeping like marmots. But the first dawn found us on our feet again and when we opened the shutters on the small chamber window, the mooing beasts came trundling in from all directions.

For us it was now a matter of making up for the lack of hospitality by “buying” when there was still no one in the shop and to disappear. The "bought" pork rinds saved us from stomach growling for a long time.

From Zarren, we drew up our additional itinerary, because we actually had to go home again now. But none of us thought of that either. We therefore agreed to meet in Brussels on a certain day to start our journey home together. Travelling without a ticket did not present any difficulties.

I chose the tour Bruges, Ostend, Ghent, Mechelen, Antwerp, Brussels. However, the war had left a different face on the cities than I remembered from my earlier trip. Nevertheless, or perhaps because of this, I found my trip very interesting. After 3 days, we found ourselves together again in Brussels, well-behaved and poor, and now drove back to Bonn, exchanging our manyfold experiences.

Later, I made the journey again, but as the attendant of a pharmacy, to the Belgian front, but it went very quickly and according to plan.

7. Whereto?

In the merry month of May, my days in the wounded company were numbered. I was fit for war again and was sent off to the reserve unit.

So now I was a candidate again and behaved accordingly. Every day I could expect to be shipped off to the front, and that made me reckless. The days, especially Sundays, had to be used to the full during this reprieve.

I wanted to realise this intention particularly strongly one Sunday at the end of May. This time, my journey went to Honnef, where I had been invited by good acquaintances to a hike in the Siebengebirge. I of course did not have any holiday. But that did not bother me. All that mattered to me was the holiday experience. I did not consider it necessary to be sanctioned by the military authorities. The time did not matter either. At 1 1/2 a.m., after a day well spent, I planned to return to Bonn. There was also a train coming, but they wouldn't let me pass the barrier.

But then my urge to go to the spacious barracks won out and I forced my way through. It must have been a bit rough in my wine mood, because I was received by the stationmaster in Beuel with the help of the station guard, had my city leave ticket revoked and was yelled at in a disgusting manner. I arrived at the barracks at 3 o'clock, tired and disheartened.

A well-known sergeant was on gate duty and wanted to smuggle me in without a fuss. In view of my experiences, however, I didn't want to do that because I thought it might draw attention to my good friend. After all it was dead certain I would be reported. So, I was entered into the guard book and would also have gotten my three days detention if Monday had not demanded more important duties of me. As soon as he arrived at the company, the loyal old Captain Rolfink asked for volunteers to transport me to the Italian front, because in the meantime the Italians could no longer be trusted.

Since my peace clock had already run out, he urged me to do this new thing. But that also atoned for my serious Sunday crime. You can't punish people like that, Rolfink said later. We got dressed in a hurry and were soon ready to march out again.

PART 2: THE EASTERN FRONT

8. The Long Way to the Regiment

Some inexplicable circumstances however delayed our departure and I still had time to bring about a final meeting with my Tilla, who toiled to make it clear that our wartime friendship wanted to be an unbreakable comradeship. We had chosen the Liebliche Lin as the place to meet. With this love in my heart, I soon left for the East. The Isonso Front and the Tagliamento and Po with that had come to nothing.

On a holiday in the first days of June, our transport train rolled through the sunny German countryside. We were our 700 men, who had thrown themselves together in Cologne.

Soldiers were still held in high esteem at that time and our richly decorated train was greeted lively everywhere. We still believed in our trip to Italy when we were already in Landsberg an der Warthe. But soon doubts began to arise as our destination became ever more easterly. We were not yet in the habit of making such detours.

And sure enough, the next afternoon we are sitting in Tilsit. Strangely enough, we

Bonners didn't have any rifles yet. But we got them here at the pouch collection point, but they were also after that.

Tilsit is a clean but charmless little town, where we 700 men were already a considerable garrison.

Unfortunately, the next morning we already had to continue our journey to the Russian border.

The first Russian town we reached was Tauroggen, which was completely destroyed. Now we followed clear war tracks for 6 days in extremely strenuous marches. The difficulties of nightly accommodation, which also had to provide food, grew daily. We did not have field kitchens with us.

The ever-changing picture of the melancholy Russian countryside captivated us very much. We have already spent 6 to 7 hours roaming through the most magnificent forests. The area of operations has a completely different character than the western front, due to the spatial limitations of the east. The destruction is also not so general. One found whole areas completely spared by the war and other stretches of land where, however, every settlement had been incinerated.

There were no developed positions, as we knew them from the west. Only knee-deep ditches and holes gave us a hint of a position.

We enjoyed beautiful evenings after a long march and feasted on the produce of the land.

On the penultimate day of our approach, we encountered cavalry. It was dragoons, who were on some mission across our path. The horsemen were not particularly communicative. They must have been extremely tired. Nor could we find out from them where our division stood.

We were now over 1000 kilometres away from home and had not seen a railway for 5 days. This feeling of the endless expanses binds the troops together, creates comradeship and the ability of one to stand up for the other.

The front made itself felt the next day. The sound of cannons and plumes of smoke clearly indicated the direction. The transports of wounded became more and more numerous. These transports were quite strange. The more or less wounded soldiers lay on little straw-covered wagons pulled by Lilliputian horses. The lightly wounded played the carters. They all looked very run-down, but their eyes shone with the dawn of the homeland peace towards which they were striving.

The landscape was quite well populated by Russian standards. We found ourselves at the Suwalki governorate.

The population practised agriculture almost exclusively, in a medieval, partly antediluvian way. The land seemed, according to its growth, to be fertile. Only wooden houses with thatched roofs could be seen.

Around noon on this last day of marching, we arrived at our division. The regiment was engaged with the advancing Russians at Ilgica, who had to cover the road back to Vilna. Exceptionally tired from the exertions of the last few days, the troops had fallen asleep, literally asleep, in their field positions.

This circumstance made it possible for the enemy to advance suddenly and a lively battle ensued, forcing our troops to retreat. There were extraordinarily heavy losses. Many troops also fell into Russian captivity.

Just at this critical moment, we entered the battlefield and were immediately engaged. But in the meantime, the field artillery had also grasped the critical situation and intervened in the battle, which had so far only been answered dimly by German riflemen. I got into the artillery cover and thus had the opportunity to observe the whole battle from a hill. There were about 100 of us at the artillery's disposal. The artillery was hitting the Russian ranks with extraordinary vehemence. Although we were able to hold our ground until evening, we retreated about 10 km at nightfall. Unfortunately, many dead and wounded were left in the panje[7] houses.

---

[7] "Russky"

We slept without tents in a dew-soaked meadow and were given field kitchen meals for the first time in the morning. Rice with apple rings was the first meal I received in Russia, and it was fine. No sooner had we finished this great service than we were off again. Now a firing line was calmly formed, and a low ridge was thrown out. My company lay in the middle of a cornfield. There was not a trace of the enemy to be noticed, let alone to be seen. Therefore, we were not in a hurry with our work, although we were repeatedly advised to hurry.

Then, suddenly, we were spotted by artillery and diligently we went into the ground. But the attack we expected did not come. It became mysteriously quiet again. No cloud of dust, no trampling of horses, no creaking of wagons, nothing was audible. So we lay for hours and let the glorious June sun, shine on us.

A spicy smell emanated from the freshly mown earth. The freshly mown grain in the field smelled even better than hay.

We were talking to the few old men (the company had only come out of the battle with 55 men) about the way the Russians were fighting and the best way to deal with them, when an airman came and looked around the area. He will not have seen much of the position, which was well covered with mown grain. The airman was brought down. During the recovery of the aircraft, two men were injured by shrapnel.

Now a Russian cavalry patrol also approached. We only gave them money after the riders, fired on by outposts, took flight. The Russians then tried to contact us again and again.

500 m in front of our cornfield, a high forest stretched for kilometres. Occasionally during a patrol, we noticed that this forest had only a small extension towards the enemy, and it seemed advisable to lay a double-post chain in the exit of the forest, which was controlled by a shuttle post. During the first night I had to perform this duty. Accordingly, we moved about 1000 m in front of the trench.

At this time of year, it is only dark for 4 hours in Russia. The transition from day to night was remarkably quick. The terrain in front of us was not particularly clear. It consisted of willow with scattered clumps of trees and shrubbery. A house was visible in the distance. The Russian did not venture further than this single house. Our cover was very extensive beech trunks.

We would have liked to know more about the Russian position and crept forward under cover of darkness with 3 men. Unobserved, we reached the height of the house and could hear the soldiers' voices well. The Russian guard fired his rifle every minute to prove that he was not asleep. We could not find a position. We did not dare to venture further.

On our return from this excursion, we received fire from our comrades because we had lost our way a little. This was intensified at our shouting until they finally realised that we were our own people. After being relieved, the shuttle guards had to report to the company commander.

When I reported, "Nothing new at the post," I got a proper rebuff because the shooting had been heard in the trench. But it had been agreed among us to keep quiet about the less than praiseworthy incident. The company leader concluded his sermon on the guards with the promise that I would soon be given patrol duty where there would be something "new" for a change.

From that night on, this company leader could no longer knock me down.

I was therefore glad when a captain arriving from home took over the company two days later. This captain had already been wounded in the storms outside Antwerp at Fort St. Katharinen.

When he inspected the company on his first walk through the trench, he spoke to each soldier. So he also asked me the following questions:

"Been out yet?"
"Yes, Captain, in the West."
"Home?"
"Bonn, Herr Hauptmann. "
"Student?"
"No, Herr Hauptmann, administrative trainee."

"War volunteer, I suppose?"
"Yes, Captain."

After this inspection I was chased by my platoon leader to the captain, who was standing in front of his dugout in a little stream valley. There were a lot of other soldiers lined up here.

The company commander briefly explained the necessity of promoting non-commissioned officers and privates in order to be able to provide the company, which had been badly hit, with suitable group leaders.

Finally, he wished to have some soldiers as messengers. However, there seemed to be no particular inclination among the enlisted men for this use.

Although I had no idea what functions this office entailed, I stepped forward.

Three more men followed me. This number seemed sufficient. Then he dismissed the entire clan except for us 4 men.

He told us that from then on, we would be inseparable. We had to take up quarters with him immediately and were only at his disposal.

So I fetched bag and baggage and moved to the stream.

Here, the four of us sniffed each other and it turned out that one of us was a businessman, one a teacher, one a musician and I, as I said, was an administrator. The first 3 had been with the regiment from the beginning, so had left in January 1915. We harmonised very well together and now built ourselves a light-covered cosy dugout, the walls of which we neatly covered with cornstalks.

Our duty consisted of taking orders to the individual platoons and fetching orders from the battalion and delivering messages to them. At night we had to take turns standing staff watch and keeping an eye on events in the company section.

So the days passed quickly without any major warlike events. Unfortunately, we were soon relieved from this quiet position.

However, the road did not take us far from our previous location. But even here it was beautiful. We were situated near an idyllic mill with a clean pond in front of it in the valley. The mill stream was fed out of it when needed. Not far from this mill stood the manor house, a simple, well-kept wooden house with a porch and steps.

We could have accommodated ourselves comfortably here. But we didn't do that, instead we built ourselves another nice shelter, to have a home when the manor house was in ruins, which could be brought about at any moment by artillery fire.

The trench ran about 30 m in front of this manor house through gardens and fields.

Next to the house were two very tall, slender maple trees. Storks had built their nest in one of them. In the other one we had an observation post, which allowed a wonderful distant view, especially as the lime tree was a bit high anyway.

I spent many an hour at this dizzy height. This situation was critical when the area was under fire. It was intended to report the position on this delicate occasion, with the danger also simultaneously having the benefit of establishing the firing line of the artillery. However, despite good binoculars, this was not possible even for the artillerymen who were often our guests.

I had brought a small kitten from the mill, where it was wandering around, into my shelter. The little animal was very cute and affectionate. It was my constant companion on my many official and non-official journeys, but it did not want to go up the tall tree. I don't know whether this was due to the two dead storks hanging halfway over the nest in the neighbouring tree.

Here in the mill of Nowopol we spent a beautiful week. Every day we bathed at least once in the clear mill pond. Someone in France should have bathed 30 metres behind the trench! We only saw Russians from a distance. Accordingly, there was very little combat activity.

This delightful stay was abruptly brought to an end. One day I received orders to scout the way for a nightly relief march to another section.

That evening I led the company to a new position.

I was not a little surprised that the night had to be chosen for the march. It was to be expected that it would be less peaceful in our new position. The next few days confirmed this assumption.

The days went by with bad weather and heavy artillery activity, which brought heavy losses. My kitten, the faithful little animal, unfortunately got lost during these days. I lamented this very much at the time.

A kind fate soon saved us from our difficult situation. The regiment (we were assigned to the Lauenstein army group with only 2 battalions) was relieved.

We took up quarters in the forest near Poikny, because the village of Poikny was no longer there. There was only a sign calling the charred heaps of beams and stone chimneys Poikny.

The forest (a coniferous forest) held beautiful arbour-like shelters made of fir brushwood and canvas shelters. Unfortunately, the thundershowers had not yet completely stopped and left no dry spot in these arbours.

But as the weather improved, the forest soon came to life.

Now, in addition, the first mail arrived for us newcomers and we were happy soldiers. It was a wonderful camp life with lots of singing and humour and little duty.

One day, however, was used for a major marching and combat exercise. It was a 3-hour walk to the Dubissa, a small river with steep, high banks.

It was a beautiful morning when we set off at the crack of dawn. I quite enjoyed these movements, because they conveyed ever-changing images of the harsh landscape. The good field kitchen was happy to cater to our increased demands on such days and served particularly good food. Unfortunately, the fields and meadows did not offer much at this time of year (June).

Fierce fighting had taken place around Dubissa at the beginning of June. We reconstructed these battles in miniature to train ourselves for such cases in future.

After a short rest in the forest solitude of Poikny, which had absolutely nothing to do with war, we were deployed again on 25 June 1915 in the sandy desert of Wysocki-Dwor. This small estate stands in a bad memory with me. Our stay in and near this backwater was so spoiled by artillery fire that we preferred to camp in the nearby forest.

Here we found peculiar Russian shelters. These round, man-deep holes in the ground resembled cisterns.

We stuck to our habit and built green summer shelters here too. But when we occasionally got fired on here in the forest, we jumped into these Russian holes.

Nevertheless, we had to mourn one death here.

We were able to give him a beautiful funeral. The grave was magnificently decorated. The helmet was put on the cross made of birch wood.

Towards evening we made our way to the sand position. A gentle, sandy ridge rose here out of the otherwise lush terrain, the crest of which our trench furrowed. The wind kept throwing up the trench, fouling the rifles with the drifting sand, so that there were always jams in the loading.

We were shelled very heavily.

Cavalry tried twice to push us out of this sandy desert, which gave us the opportunity to observe the beautiful village of Bokrishova.

We took up this position twice as a relief. Here, rather in the Wysocki-Dwor estate, I received the first parcel post that had been trailing behind me for so long. But Panje Russki had to spoil even this momentous hour of receiving mail for me with his thick chunks of artillery bombardment. It was so intense that I ended up running through the fruit fields to the forest with numerous parcels under my arm, and that on my name day.

Finally, a decent supply of cigarettes, that was worth a lot.

One Sunday morning, we were ordered to depopulate a large part of the area of operations. It was a sad task to chase these people, happy to have escaped the dangers of war, from their homes and farms. We set a desolate caravan in motion around noon. Hastily packed meagre belongings were loaded onto equally meagre vehicles and up and away hurried small and large. The remaining livestock limped along behind the shaky wagons. Women and children squatted on the vehicles of all kinds.

"Man still sends back a glance to the grave of his possessions".

We comforted the departing men with the prospect that the imminent progress of the battle would allow them to return in a few days.

Our East Prussian brothers also met this fate at the beginning of the war.

How happy our relatives were that we had succeeded in keeping the German soil free of the enemy almost without exception.

The experiences of this sand position were followed by days of advance fighting, where the Russians always broke out in front of us. The daily skirmish was followed by quiet in the evening. At night, the front was eerily silhouetted against the burning and smouldering villages. There were no quarters, of course. We always camped near Mother Green.

We messengers had a lot of walking to do. Attempts to relieve ourselves by using bicycles failed because of the trackless terrain. Nevertheless, I rode around for weeks on a lady's bicycle, a rare prize in Russia.

When, a village ahead, we wanted to provide water relief for the thirsty troops with our bikes, we tied mop ropes from the saddle to the handlebars and back again, and then countless field bottles dangled from these ropes, which we quickly filled and brought to the company. If the nests were inhabited, the farmers had to put wooden buckets with water by the road.

We always had a hard time with these farmers because communication was difficult. If we were the first German troops to enter a village, we usually found no inhabitants. They hid fearfully. Only when they realised that we were not man-eaters, as the Cossacks had told them, did they become more trusting.

I was always amazed by the primitiveness of these people. They lived in an unimaginably simple way. Even the tools of their mostly agricultural labour were pre-medieval in simplicity. The craftsman's house was marked by hanging a boot, a butter churn, a wooden bucket, and so on. Labelling was only common in the cities.

The simple houses in the countryside, built of wood and thickly thatched, usually had 3 rooms. In the middle was the kitchen with an open fireplace and chimney, and on either side was a room-like dungeon, one of which housed the extensive oven. This oven was built in such a way that it offered space for the family members to spend the night. In the cold winter months, the whole family would squat here, fully clothed. Small livestock also roamed around happily in the living quarters. These were "domestic animals" in the true sense of the word.

The people were obviously trying to keep us from accessing their supplies. They were masters at hiding their things; burying them being the leading method. But we soon turned out to be quite resourceful treasure diggers.

In July, the battles around Janischki developed in connection with the encirclement of the Vilnius fortress. The Russians defended themselves relatively well and gave us a lot of trouble. Tremendous marches were necessary in these hot days, for the short summers in Russia are remarkably hot. Thunderstorms are a rarity in Russia. We jokingly called ourselves the "running-running division" because of the zealous marching. The ever-changing landscapes and the manifold impressions made these days a profound experience for me. Our losses were correspondingly low in the relatively mild exercise of war craft. They only increased considerably during the battles around Schaulen.

Slowly but surely, we carried forward our attacks against Swienta until we came to a standstill here at the beginning of August.

The Vilna garrison pushed impetuously out of its grip against the Dina, a broad stream that pours into the Gulf of Riga.

9. Battle of Kowarsk

For my company, 13 August 1915 was the day with the heaviest losses of the entire advance since 9 June.

In front of the small town of Kowarsk, we had relieved the cavalry in their less than useful trenches on 2 August. The position was on a gently sloping ridge. In front of us lay the town of Kowarsk with a sugar factory in its soft image and behind us stretched the extensive outworks (agricultural farm buildings) of Formannskajo.

Something could be done with this outstanding position and in a few days we had built a very good field fortification with almost bomb-proof shelters.

The small town, situated in the Swienta valley, was alternately occupied by an outpost company, which put out its feelers to the sugar factory and the river. The retreat road Vilna Dünaburg was about 18 km away. In the meantime, the cavalry had extended the mobile wide arc to the left of our army wing.

For the Russians, this threatening approach became a strong danger.

Understandable, therefore, were the desperate raids they dared to make again and again in order not to let the beautiful, wide retreat road come into our hands.

On 9 August, we had to occupy the town. The company relieved in broad daylight. A sign that, with a little caution, the stay in this outpost was bearable. We took up quarters with the company leader in the vicarage, which was adjacent to the magnificent church with its gilded onion domes, situated on a plateau. A well-tended garden surrounded the clean, spacious house. I loved the bright glass veranda with the library behind it. I sat here for many an hour and poked around in the few German works. At the end of the garden, hidden under the walnut bushes, was the little bathhouse. You couldn't tell what it was for if you had no idea what the Russians meant by a bath. This little house was used as an observation post, because from here one had a good view over the riverbed. We had to provide the lookout. One platoon of the company lay in the church, which was surrounded by a rubble stone wall. A layer of bricks formed the end of the wall. Some of the stones had been pushed away. This created embrasures. What a strong castle! The wall was crowned by 13 station houses in which a man could comfortably stand upright. These houses, as far as they faced the enemy, were made into small bastions.

It was quiet for the first two days. At night we set fire to some houses to keep some visibility. Life was good, everyone cooked a feast in addition to the good food from the field kitchen. Wine had also been found in the abandoned sexton's cottage. The Formannskajo fuel factory provided strong schnapps. What more could one want?

Unfortunately, this tranquillity did not last long.

On 12 August I was at my post late in the evening. Thanks to the telephone connection with the two platoons, reporting duty was practically superfluous. The captain visited me at my post. He followed his orders with reflections on the wonderful peacefulness of the evening and expressed his particular inner turmoil. I did not share his fears but was glad that it was so pleasantly quiet. Meanwhile, the captain had been right.

The following day began with a fierce barrage. The hits, however, were in the part of the city stretching towards our front line. It soon became apparent that the telephone lines to our trains were also interrupted. At the same time we heard heavy rifle fire and roaring from our 1st platoon, which was accommodated on the river side at the exit of the city. Immediately the 2nd platoon, located near the sugar factory, also joined in the action with rifle fire. It was a terrible confusion. Immediately afterwards, parts of our platoon came running through the town with the wildest stories about what was happening at the town exit. Some of the fellows arrived without weapons, even without helmets, and with their backs open as if deranged. They were all caught at the church and put into the 3rd platoon.

Gradually it became clear that the 1st Platoon must have been trapped by the Russians. They must have sneaked into the village at night. The 2nd Platoon, however, had correctly recognised the critical situation and rushed to the aid of the 1st Platoon. The company commander also sent half of our 3rd Platoon to meet the harassed comrades. We did not dare to expect reinforcements from the front, which was 500 to 800 m away from us. The Russian artillery masterfully managed to lay a barrage on us and our rear area up to the main position, so that no reinforcements could get through.

Soon the remnants of the 1st and parts of the 2nd and 3rd platoons returned. They also stayed with us so that we could extend our position across the market, which was in front of the church square. The row of houses on one side of the market was occupied.

The Russians pressed on cautiously. We saw the first riflemen approaching through the gardens. The hawthorn hedges gave them good cover. But when we had the riflemen directly in front of us and at the same time the artillery fire was more withdrawn, we began with murderous rifle fire from the churchyard wall. The Russians were stunned. The heavy guys threw themselves down, retreated behind the first protective hedges and banged away for all they were worth. But the Russians came rolling in in ever greater numbers.

Now they also tried to get to the market to attack our little fortress from behind. But there they also encountered difficulties. They could not get out of the houses. At the short distances of 30 to 80 metres, almost every shot was accurate, despite the excitement. Unfortunately, we also suffered some casualties, only head injuries, because the wall offered protection, but for effective shooting the heads had to protrude over the edge of the wall.

Our artillery now intervened energetically, even without knowing exactly where we were.

At least this had the effect that the Russian reinforcements arrived only sporadically. Unfortunately, German shells also hit our ranks. In the meantime, our base was only manned by about 50 men. The situation became even more desperate when the Russians crossed the Swienta River with their forces, which were still small for the time being, and also rolled up the position at the sugar factory on the other side of the town and were able to surround us from there. The company commander therefore ordered us to turn off to a slope to the east of the sugar factory. This was the most favourable connection to the main position.

I was still able to bring this order to the market. When I returned to the church square, I found only a few riflemen left. That's when I got the call from the company commander, who was standing behind the church. When I got to the command post, the captain was no longer to be seen. I now looked over the wall and saw him running with 3 men through the gardens towards the river. The rest of the cemetery crew was pushing towards the houses at the market, from where I had just come. I threw my knapsack into a corner, my carbine over the wall and hurriedly followed. I quickly grabbed a folded blanket that

I saw lying on the ground and soon caught up with the captain and the three men.

Now we went from one house to the other, always under fire from the enemy riflemen who were crossing the river. Here, of all places, we had the longest way to the main position.

With our skins intact we reached the new cemetery, which was adjacent to the ridge occupied by our regiment. This cemetery was also enclosed by a low quarry stone wall. Here, for the time being, we could take a breather under the protection of the strong wall. But this could not last long, for we were not in a position to set up for a defence here.

The peculiarity of the Russian cemeteries served us well here. We were able to seek shelter behind the heavy 4 to 5 m high oak crosses as we retreated. But we didn't have far to go to reach the NCO post on a terrace-like ledge. We reached it without any damage. The 8 men dug in here had been busy shooting down the Russians who were crossing the river. That was our salvation. That we now also joined in the shooting was a matter of course. A short breather in this trench allowed us to handle our weapons safely again. Like on the shooting range it went here: fingers long, set down. And we had a grim rage in our cheeks.

The captain didn't suffer here for long. He wanted to join the battalion staff. So we discussed how best to get over the mountain. As safe as we felt here in the deep trench, the way over the mountain, seen by the enemy, was also difficult. We finally agreed to try a run one at a time. I was to go first. That was fine with me, because I thought that before the Panjes had even set up to make a retrograde "foundation" here, you would be over there. I was almost over the nose when the first bullets clapped in beside me. It had worked. Soon the captain arrived too. With his girth and age, plus the thigh injury, that was quite a feat for him. The three other comrades stayed behind at the sergeant's post for the time being. That was the arrangement after I had made my jump.

Now we were soon at the battalion and the artillery also received the long-awaited information. Unfortunately, we did not know exactly whether the remnants of the company had already been able to follow the order to evade before the Russians surrounded the town. This gave the artillery cause to spare the town itself. Afterwards it turned out that 55 men had found the right way.

However, the main position was not attacked, as was now expected. The Russians remained stuck in the nest and were neatly spotted. In the evening, with few exceptions, the houses were in flames.

Our company had lost 1 officer and nearly 100 men. Of these, the officer and 28 men had been taken prisoner, as we learned later.

The Russians had dragged the wounded into a synagogue - a wooden house. This house, as we were assured by one of these wounded, who was discovered and rescued at night in the willow bushes by the stream, had been set on fire by ruffians. The one we had rescued had fled from the building, exerting the last of his energy.

We later found this incredible news actually confirmed by many uniform buttons and waist hooks on the scene of the fire.

The 10th Company was now replenished from the stocks of the remaining 7 Companies. We did not get the best soldiers in this way.

The next night, a bold patrol undertook to ransack the nest once. The people also came as far as the market, as they credibly stated. It turned out that the Russian town was held only by weak cavalry forces.

On 16 August, early in the morning, we received the order to reoccupy. As a result of good preparations, the surprise succeeded with few casualties.

In one of the few remaining houses, potatoes were still boiling on the fire, as was the gruel soup that the Russians liked to eat.

We found our dead only superficially covered, where they were lying, in garden and field, they had been buried. Some piece of wood with a helmet on it, also a sunflower, marked the hero's grave.

We stayed in Kowarsk for three more days. Clean shelters had already been built, but we moved on.

10.Deployment to the Battle of Daugavpils

The river was crossed by means of a makeshift bridge made of planks resting on barrels, baskets and bundles of rushes. Of course, field kitchens, cartridge wagons and guns, even of light calibre, could not be brought across. It was not a particularly pleasant feeling to have to make an advance without artillery cover. In front of us unknown terrain and the uncertainty about the enemy's type and strength, and behind us the river with this single shaky bridge. If necessary, we could swim through the water. Then we were standing over on the other side without weapons and could not even defend ourselves against the pursuers.

By noon we were engaged with weak enemy forces near the village of Doginze at the confluence of the Gara River and the Swienta. The undulating terrain made our advance much easier. And already the 9th Company was sitting in the village, which had been abandoned by the fleeing enemy almost without a fight, with a loud hurrah.

We took up quarters in the forest. The 9th Company naturally remained in the captured village. Several kilometres of patrols gave us the certainty that the new situation was not to be taken tragically.

Here on the little river Gara we led a nice Robinson life.

The well-established potato fields gave us the opportunity to bake a good batch of potato pancakes. A pan was quickly found in the village. Some women who had found their way back to their houses after the battle, despite threats from the Russians, were supposed to provide a grater. I could not communicate well with the women. They didn't understand even the clearest sign language. Afterwards I helped myself by cutting open a large tin can, drilling holes in it and fixing it to a board. I punched the holes into the tin with a steel clamp. Now the women knew what I wanted and there were plenty of potato graters to be had. As we gathered for a good feast, replacements arrived from home. Twenty timid soldiers and an old sergeant, all newcomers. Under the circumstances, they had soon settled in with us.

The three of us were suddenly torn apart. One of the three fell ill with encephalitis and the other, my friend Kumps, the teacher, was ordered to the officers' course. Our best, Private B., had been lost to us earlier. His departure had nothing to do with warlike events. He had been sent to Tilsit on 2 July with the baggage of fallen officers of the regiment and then, giving in to his recklessness, never returned. He had squandered the money he had been given to buy tobacco, cigarettes and other useful things. At the end of September he was brought back to us as a swindler by two Berlin sergeants.

It was hard for me to say goodbye to Kumps. We had shared everything with each other and had become very close on the many reporting tours. The company commander chose two new reporting officers. He made a choice that also satisfied me. The new replacement was a customs officer trainee who spoke reasonable Russian and Polish. We really needed this guy. So he became a dispatcher. The second "newcomer" was a merchant. He had been with the company for a long time.

At the beginning of September we gave up the position, which was not really a position at all, because there was no more fighting at all.

The Russians' Great Retreat Road to Dünaburg was reached in a few morning hours. We camped in the ditch. Here I experienced for the first time the gigantic picture of the deployment of an entire army group. For hours I was interested in the diversity of the army procession. The troops were in extremely good spirits. The attempt to find any acquaintances during the advance was in vain. There seemed to be only two kinds of soldiers: those with moustaches and those without. I had the idea of looking over the roadside at the soldiers' feet, the horses' legs and the rotating wheels of the vehicles. In a relatively short time, this had the effect that I fell asleep despite the considerable wheel noise.

The march was the prelude to the battle in front of Dünaburg.

It goes without saying that I was roused early to take part in this battle.

On 9 September 1915, our regiment was involved in the battle at Leljuny. The fighting around Dünaburg, a remarkable fortress, was more intense than we were used to in the battles around Schaulen, Pärmmewitach and Rupischki, considering the many possibilities of the Russians with their base in the background. The artillery activity on both sides had increased to such an extent that we could no longer speak of a comfortable war.

The Russians had built exceptionally good field fortifications with the help of the civilian population and prisoners of war. These positions were usually stacked on top of each other. The trenches were securely covered against shrapnel fire. Branch and wire entanglements were carefully and amazingly extensive. In addition, the numerous large and small lakes around Dünaburg naturally offered obstacles.

Therefore, the most favourable points of attack for us had to be selected in order to limit the losses to the lowest possible level. This tactic, which our leader at the time, Hindenburg, mastered, naturally required all kinds of evasive marches and mock manoeuvres.

At Leljuny, we succeeded in breaking through the front at a less strong point and pushed on and rolled up with extraordinary force and speed. But the Russians also knew their weaknesses and had appropriate interception positions ready, which caused us a lot of grief.

One such position blocked the already narrow passage between two lakes in front of Leljuny. The terrain was also swampy to a good extent, so that only a narrow pass remained for the advance. Our situation was really critical and forced us to fight desperately. The rush in the narrow space caused great loss. Then suddenly the field artillery pushed forward into our firing lines and a frenzied shooting started. In a short time we had taken the Russian position by storm.

The Russians did not engage in hand-to-hand combat, but stuck their rifles with their dirty, rusty, square-edged sidearms into the ground and surrendered with a great roar. Officers were rarely present.

The steadfastness of the Russian troops was often dependent on their tribal affiliation. The Poles, for example, were not worth very much. The Baltic regiments, on the other hand, fought extraordinarily stubbornly. The much-feared Cossacks were rarely to be found in the front. As police troops, they mostly harassed the hinterland.

This hot day of fighting was followed by an equally hot day at Antalogi on 10 September. Here we did not come to blows until late in the evening. In the darkness, we had run ourselves into each other's "yarns" in an outwork not far from Antalogi. Germans had been shooting at Germans all the time.

The morning before this battle I had another funny experience. We had occupied a bridgehead at about 10 o'clock. A small trench was quickly dug and some trip wire was strung, then we were idle and craving milk and honey. Ahead of us, by the stream, lay a small estate. I obtained permission from the platoon leader to whom I was assigned to inspect the homestead for food. Two men went with me. There was still bread there. A potting bench also contained several pots of milk. I wanted to be modest and took the smallest pot. It held about 1 1/2 measures. The others contained 5 measures. We took as much bread as we could carry. The two comrades also took a large pot of milk. We proudly arrived with our booty. When the distribution went on, it turned out that I had captured cream and the other two soured milk, which only had a small layer of cream.

What a breakfast: chunks of bread and cream!

Those who could not be included in the distribution also tried a requisition and afterwards we had all enjoyed good refreshment. Unfortunately, the breakfast did not have the expected effect. It was too much of a good thing. In addition to my official walks, I had to make many "private walks".

On 11 September, we reached the cute little town of Uziany, situated on a large, clear lake, without a fight. The joy of the forthcoming quarters in the little town ahead of us lifted our spirits tremendously. Unfortunately, the beautiful quarters had to be vacated again after two hours.

Shoulder your rifles!
Without a step, march!

Oh, how cruel!

Towards evening we were in action again. But then my company was pulled out of the front and spent the night with the brigade staff.

Early in the morning of the following September 12, the battle began at Dusjaty, a town inhabited by numerous Jews, also situated on a lake. Here we took many prisoners. Unfortunately, our stay here was also very short. We were not at all pleased that our "descendants" should now enjoy everything that we had actually "conquered".

We reached Schunelki on the same day. But now the proximity of the Dünaburg bridgehead became noticeable. The progress was no longer as fast. Fliers became more numerous. Very heavy artillery made life difficult for us with its extraordinarily thick chunks. In addition, we were very exhausted. Rations came to us only irregularly. If we had luckily dragged a field kitchen along due to good road conditions, then there were no products and we had to "get" potatoes, vegetables and meat. These vegetable soups, which contained everything that did not put up a fight, were simply delicious.

On 14 September, a brief skirmish developed in front of Mukule Castle. Only a few shots were exchanged. Once the artillery had properly radioed in, the Russians, they were "dragoons", gave up the weak resistance altogether. Two platoons of our company had developed in firing line from the outworks and were already in the castle park when I received orders to report to the advancing troops that a halt was to be made at the end of the park.

I had just pulled down a respectable branch from a Reineclauden[8] tree when I was ordered to start trotting.

I didn't want to miss out on the tasty fruit. Dragging the branch unsuspectingly behind me, I dashed off in the direction of the castle. Of course, we continued to eat quietly. I have always been so proud to call it a castle. The Russians were a bit careless with this designation. What was marked on the map as Mukule Castle could have been called a country house. Well, let's call it a castle. For me, this thing has become more important than all the other castles I saw later in Russia.

As I walked cheekily through the castle, a Russian as tall as a tree jumped down the veranda steps on the garden side and ran through the orchard. Heavy apple and pear trees stood in this garden. Needless to say I was shocked beyond measure that a Russian suddenly appeared in front of me.

My fruit rice was forgotten. I pulled down the carabiner and shouted: Stoi, Panje!

---

[8] Renekloden (Prunus domestica ssp italica), also called Reineclauden , is a subspecies of the plum

Freeze! - Niema poof - there's no shooting - that was a shot.

The Russian seemed to want to stop too. He looked around and I expected him to stick his rifle in the ground, but suddenly the guy ran on, jumped behind one of the thick tree trunks and laid into me. That was the end of my patience. I leaned my gun on a flower bench on the veranda in front of me and there was a bang.

The Russian fell with a strange jolt into a ditch running along the wide gravel path. Despite my understandable excitement, he had received the first shot, in the right hip, as I later discovered when I brought him help with two medics. First, I had to bring my order forward. The indescribable look the seriously wounded Russian gave me, haunted me for a long time. Until then, I had never seen a human being so directly in front of the shotgun.

We occupied the position near Mukule for several days. Since the area was being shelled, we stayed with the company in the park that bordered the orchard.

The house still contained all kinds of rarities. We stole a gramophone with records. We carried it around for another two years. There was also a fine fur coat. I took it and made a tent out of it. When the captain saw my tent, he asked me if I knew what precious garment I had there. I gently hinted that I could only call life precious. All the trimmings would have lost the spice of preciousness in the war. The instruction that my humble tent roof was a Persian coat did not make the slightest impression on me, who had not the faintest idea of Persians.

The swampy terrain in front of us made the attack, which was deemed necessary, quite impossible. This was also recognised by the regimental commander Heck, who had previously, without knowing the difficulties, reproached the battalion commander von Köckeritz for not being available for an assault. But in order to facilitate the attack of our neighbours on the right and left, we made a mock attack at dawn on 19 September with much fanfare and a mad dash of shooting.

The Germans succeeded, as usual. Unfortunately, a good acquaintance from the home village of my blessed mother, whom I had welcomed as a regimental comrade for the first "and last time" at the lake of Uziany, was killed. He served with the 5th Company.

The success of the action made it unnecessary for us to remain here. The company left around noon in battalion formation. I had to find the office, the kitchen and the cartridge car as well as the usual light combat baggage and bring them back.

When you've been wandering around for half a day and have finally found your way with a lot of effort, you can be furious when the troops receive the order to leave just as they arrive. This trick of fate hit me particularly hard here, because it was an endless night march that followed my long way without interruption. A farmer who had been picked up as a guide turned out to be an extraordinary troll who had apparently never been beyond the boundary of his parish.

The whole night was spent marching and swearing and marching and swearing, not counting a short break in a burning village.

On the following day, however, we were able to enjoy an extended rest after only half an hour of skirmishing. We rested and ate our fill, moved to Imbrody on 22 September 1915, and from here we pressed on in a light fight to the railway line Wilna - Dünaburg.

Our destination was supposed to be the Berghof railway station. In wild haste we crossed the railway embankment and also threw the Russians out of a farmstead about 2 km behind Berghof. This farm was on a hill. We should have stayed away. The one day of our possession did not make us happy. We had many casualties at this exposed post and had to go back to straighten the front.

In this estate we got back our friend Baldus, the runaway. The extra tour cost him seven years in the fort after the court martial.

The march to the railway line had taken place with quite some speed. Stragglers, called battle bummers, now tried to reach the battalion again in their comfortable gait. But as we had meanwhile made the turn, because the wings did not come up, the unfortunates got into no man's land here and were caught by the Russian cavalry.

Our way now also went to Smelina on the main road to Dünaburg. Then we were stranded in front of the fortress. We could go no further. Fierce fighting broke out around the lake belt of Lawkessa Lake - Dryswiaty Lake - Medum Lake and the many small lakes.

The extraordinarily hard fighting, reminiscent of the French war of position, did not bring us the final success we had hoped for in view of the onset of winter. The fighting, which lasted until about November 1 and took place in the Medum and Krivoy-Most areas, forced the Russians into positions that seemed less dangerous to us, but that was the end of it. We were able to secure dominating heights and wooded positions in any case.

Directly adjacent to the big road, the companies lay in a forest position near Lake Medum towards the end of October.

Our casualties were occasionally exceptionally heavy.

The dugouts offered no substantial protection against the heavy calibre projectiles from the fortress. Our constant contact with the enemy cost us several prisoners. We also lost our interpreter here. But we also succeeded in capturing a large number of Russians. Sometimes a shout was enough to pave the way for the war-weary Russians to join us.

The good condition of the army road also enabled our army command to bring forward the heaviest guns. We owed the increase in the number of prisoners mainly to their devastating effect.

At Medum Sea I experienced the first night-time Zeppelin action against the fortress of Dünaburg. A gigantic spectacle that filled us all with pride.

The extraordinary demands made on the troops in the position battle in front of Dünaburg required relief at intervals of 4 - 5 days. A type of combat was in practice, as was the case at the focal points of the Western Front.

The resting position was Smelina. Here, however, we were not completely detached from the fighting, for nothing had to be done to lay or improve extensive wire entanglements and exemplary trenches with almost bomb-proof shelters in the front.

On 1 November 1915, our company leader, Captain Diebert, left us. He became the leader of a Landsturm battalion. It was not easy for him and us to say goodbye. After all, we lost in him a prudent, faithful leader.

The new company leader was a lieutenant who came directly from the Trier garrison. He was an elderly, somewhat scrawny gentleman with a long, thin moustache. In his civilian job he was the mayor of a small town in the Bergisches Land. We had not gotten a good bargain in him. His practical experience was understandably very limited.

When the company was presented to him, he saw three musketeers standing in front. This must have seemed very untidy to him, and he therefore asked a sergeant what the appendage was. He did not know what to make of the answer that it was 3 orders receivers. However, he believed he could do without our 3 services and placed us in the company.

The first snow covered the whole of Russia, and on 3 November the Russians, supported by the energy of Baltic regiments, were able to break through our neighbouring position occupied by the Landwehr. Since we were in "rest", we had to jump into the breach right away with other formations. However, the days had already been corrected when we had almost reached our marching objective. The dicey situation, however, necessitated our remaining on standby. On this occasion, however, the necessity of the reporting service became openly apparent.

The three of us therefore resumed our duties.

However, it was not possible to accommodate the troops in quarters, so the night had to be spent in the open with a campfire. The snow incessantly covered the sleepers at the extinguished fires when I returned from my reconnaissance of suitable quarters. The scene was harrowing yet beautiful.

The new company commander's special suitability became clearly apparent when we had to intervene in the battle at Lake Ilsen the following day. The gentleman's nervousness soon spread to the whole company without exception.

In the evening, when we had gained a foothold in a forest in the dripping rain that had replaced the snowfall, he had an earthen hut built for himself and lay down with the three of us to sleep. He did not post any guards. The guards of the company did not know his hut. Nor was there any other connection that would have guaranteed a connection with his company in the impenetrable darkness of the night.

As luck would have it, the company had to leave in the middle of the night. Since no company leader could be found, they did so without him.

My comrade Neschen was not a little surprised the next morning when he crawled out of the hole in the ground and found the company's hastily prepared pine huts destroyed and abandoned. He didn't dare tell the company leader the news but called me out. When I too had recognised the situation, I reported the strange state of affairs to the high lord. As if stung by a tarantula, he jumped out of his wigwam, wiped his eyes and began to nag. He could not get it into his head that his company could leave without his order, simply without him.

But what was the use of all that nagging, we had to see that we could re-join them. Finally, however, the old man became meek and wanted advice on what to do.

It was a funny scene, the four perplexed people in the lonely morning forest, not knowing where to go.

In order to do something, it was decided that I should try to keep a lookout on the bare mountain ridge visible from the edge of the forest. But the old man would not let me go alone. So he went with me.

It was difficult to make progress in the soggy ground. The considerable mountain gave us a fairly wide view, but neither German nor Russian troops were to be seen far and wide.

Silent warfare does not exist generally.

So I could have spared myself further action. Nevertheless, I decided to go down into the plain, which was covered with a lot of low shrubbery, to ascertain any tracks. Suddenly, during my cautious march, I heard footsteps and rustling, which prompted me to stop and determine the cause.

The safety catch on my carbine was already flying to off when I saw the lone hiker in front of me forcing his way through the wet bushes. It was a gunnery sergeant who was a news officer, as he said. I learned from him that no German heart was beating for miles around. The front had long since been brought forward again. I went back with him to the company leader on the hilltop and with a little more hope we moved back together to the forest.

We were lucky; after a short time we came across the combat baggage in the forest. The kitchens were bogged down in the soft forest soil and we eagerly helped to bring these valuable cannons over the slippery path.

At noon we were at the battalion. We did not receive any special award for this extra tour. Even the face of the company commander did not suggest to me that the encounter had been particularly affectionate.

In the evening we moved into a muddy position and stayed there for two days. Then we were relieved by Landwehr and returned to Smelina.

In mid-December, the 1st Battalion of the regiment arrived here, which had remained in Poland in June at Wariampol, Kalwaria and Sejni and had spent the entire summer and autumn fighting in another army unit.

11.Two-Year Position

The section that now fell to us on the Duna front was south of the road along the Lawkessa creek in heavily wooded hilly country.

If someone had told us when we took possession of Polishki and Shkichava: We will stay here for almost two years, we would have laughed at him.

And yet we held the position from 17 November 1915 until the end of August 1917. We were not even relieved.

What we were spared in the months that followed in terms of warlike hardships, the barbaric Russian winter gave us with full hands.

The dugouts offered little protection against this savage fellow. It was good that there was plenty of wood in the place.

The great distance from the enemy and the lack of visibility of our heavily wooded, hilly position made it possible to burn any kind of fuel.

Such a Russian winter with its eternal snow naturally has its charms for a nature lover.

The terrible frost of 25-30 degrees brought intensive position building to a standstill. Our main occupation was to clean the trenches, which were always covered with snow, and to stand guard. A trench or listening post at that time bore no resemblance to a soldier. Wrapped in a long fur coat, felt boots on their feet, two or three head protectors wrapped around them, the polar bears stood there tramping incessantly from one leg to the other. A constant replacement of the guards reduced the standby times.

How we enjoyed the army rum during this time. It got us around the many cliffs of that winter with its wild magic.

The Russians, accustomed to dirt, wanted to take advantage of the melting snow at the end of March 1916 to open their hostilities. In doing so, they also ventured close to our position. But they were smothered in dirt and crossfire. The rebuff was so thorough that they left us alone for months.

My military passport simply records these battles as "March battles in front of Dünaburg". But what they demanded in terms of toil and sacrifice can only be said by those who had to trudge around in this deluge of mud and snow water.

After these stormy days, I went home on leave from the Eastern Front for the first time. Children, what an experience it is to make the pilgrimage from this eastern dirt and mud over icy roads that flooded with snow water to a real railway train and then ever closer to home, to finally see home lying on the Rhine in a sea of blossoms. Is that fine!

The cup of holiday joy was savoured to the full.

Once the days were happily spent, then it was back again without a grumble.

The good weather that came towards the end of April gave us the opportunity to put the position into a condition that allowed us to manage with few forces, because the West had become so extremely hungry for replacements.

The shortage of men was met by the use of numerous machine guns. For example, we had 12 M.G.s in our company. Most of them were of Russian origin. They rested on small wheels and were very handy. They were used to equip the many nests, which were laid out with great skill. We also had a small-calibre cannon fitted. They were supposed to spout cartridges.

Great attention was also paid to path construction. The swampy areas were provided with billet dams. The bottom of the trench was also given wooden grates. The trench walls were neatly covered with 8 to 12 cm thick wooden logs. The intelligence service erected lines in three forms: a well-insulated overhead line, a line along fir poles about 10 - 15 cm thick that ran about 1/2 m above the ground and a carefully covered underground line about 20 cm in the ground.

It is therefore easy to imagine the enormous amount of work that was necessary for the decimated crew to carry out in addition to their post duties.

The material depots showed an abundance of cement, timber, boards and corrugated iron. The front gobbled all this up with a greedy mouthful.

In the meantime, the leadership of the company had passed into other hands. If at the beginning we had met the new company leader, who came from the cavalry, with a certain mistrust, we soon had to revise our opinion in view of the excellent soldierly and comradely qualities of the new master. He led us with much circumspection and a correctness which, applied to the whole arm, should have led to the best understanding between troop and leader. We had the opportunity to draw comparisons with our neighbouring companies and were pleased to find that in this respect everything was in perfect order. Accordingly, the atmosphere amongst us was unsurpassable and led to a noble competition in performance and comradeship.

The combat activity in the spring and summer did not go beyond the usual amount of position fighting.

One fine day I was sitting on the roof garden of my dugout on the steep slope behind the trench, nicely ornamented with birch trunks, when the company commander came sauntering along with his fox and dragged me to the 2nd platoon. There he thrusts his binoculars into my hand and points to freshly thrown-up yellow mounds in the shaggy foothills of the Russian position. Between us and the Russians lay a wooded hollow with a clear stream flowing through it. The terrain was confusing. The undergrowth had not yet been excessively cleared by shelling. I had to explain to the chief what the yellow spots were all about. My verdict was: "Herr Leutnant, it is a matter of some random but somewhat irregular new shell impacts, which could give the erroneous impression that a small ditch has been placed under our noses overnight". "Misfired", came the reply, adding the common term for a desert ship, "that is in fact a new trench". I stand by my intemperate opinion, which the platoon leader did not dare to endorse, although he also shared it.

The company commander ordered that the new trench be dug in the evening. He himself wanted to lead the violent reconnaissance. Since we had been lying on the bear skin for a long time, the fighting spirit revived in some of us. Therefore, 25 men volunteered for the planned undertaking. The battalion gave its consent in the afternoon and by nightfall we were ready with pistols and hand grenades. A council of war was held, and it was finally decided that 9 men would go from the south and 9 men from the north and push the Russians towards the centre of the supposed new ditch. The company commander, a non-commissioned officer and I had to proceed silently from the extension trench directly against the trench section and take up positions in a former listening post hole. At 9.05 sharp, the two groups had to leave their agreed starting point. The artillery observer was present and initiated. When our comrades shook hands and wished us good luck, that ticklish feeling crept up our spines that creeps over us when, somewhat weaned from the scuffle, we are supposed to approach the enemy again after everything has been prepared and talked about for hours.

Last but not least, we had to have a slogan. This was hastily taken from our most common vocabulary and was called "Shoot".

So we Indians set off without a belt and rifle. The cap was put on with the visor to the back. As I said, we only had pistols and hand grenades as weapons, plus the small spade.

It was one of those beautiful, quiet evenings when even the smallest sound of the battle front could be heard. One could hear the creaking of wheels in the rutted paths behind the front on both sides. Even the confused voices of the soldiers were audible and the clatter of cooking utensils. Quiet as if with utmost decency, the three of us squatted in our crumbling listening post hole and peered into the fateful night. Such a quarter of an hour's anticipation is something delicate. What a wealth of fleeting thoughts whiz through the hot head. Life's strange milestones flashed by like a panorama and one is inclined to quickly add one's own little crude cross to the end of the picture.

All of a sudden, the dance starts, and the nerves are already reconnected to the new situation, which is in urgent need of them. The northern group has already met resistance in its approach. The weak Russian patrol backs away and slams into the terrain randomly and haphazardly. Now the southern group is also experiencing fierce rattling.

Hand grenades were already bursting over there. So they are closer. The northern group is attacked by stronger Russian forces who jump in to help the patrol. The bright crash of hand grenades to the south of us increases. The supposed trench in front of us is shrouded in mysterious silence. We have not yet noticed that the enemy forces have been squeezed by our two groups in front of us. If we don't stalk ahead soon, we probably wouldn't get any reconnaissance on the trench section. So, legs in hand and out we go. We reach the heights and find, as I had assessed, some shell holes and no trench. Who was now the camel was not discussed in the hurry. The Russians did not allow themselves to be crowded together, they pulled back the harassed wings a little and attacked frontally. Therefore, the groups broke away again, pushing towards the centre. When we stumbled back from our advance, we clashed with parts of these groups and got some more hand grenades in front of us. Behind an uprooted fir tree, which I was using as cover, a hand grenade fragment hit me directly above the pulse in my right arm and neck. But the slogan soon cleared up the messed-up comrades. Even before we reached the extension-trench head, our artillery fire began and brought some more confusion into our ranks. With the exception of three men, we were all back. The Russians had been rooted out by this little action like an anthill stirred up with a club. The 3 men who were left behind, soon managed to find their way back safely through thick and thin. Almost all of us had received some kind of scratch or bump. Over a bottle of schnapps, the evening's bush war was discussed once more and put on file. No crosses needed to be made this time.

Since my actual functions as a dispatcher became almost superfluous and I wanted to wrest as much interest as possible from the monotony of the war of position, I tried my hand at learning various military specialities.

One after the other, I took part in M.G. courses, mine-thrower exercises, close combat training, telephone service, indicator-, signaller-, sound meter service and finally ended up with the 47th Field Aviation Division to try my hand at this weapon as well.

However, I ran into a corner. My heart defect denied me the satisfaction of this wish. The two beautiful summer months I spent in the castle not far from Uziany will therefore remain unforgettable to me.

It was also here that I received the Iron Cross one day and was made a regular private.

In the autumn of 1916, fierce fighting began again in our section. We were now able to survive the sometimes very fierce cannonades in our bomb-proof dugouts, which had 5 to 6 m of grown earth above them, with all the peace of mind we could muster.

As is well known, the winter of 1916/17 was particularly defiant. The increase in grimness of this winter - it was 30 / 35 degrees cold - we now had better accommodation to counteract.

I took the favourable opportunity to learn how to ski in a 14-day course.

Our training terrain was the bare heights near Rowo-Alexandrovsk, where I took up quarters with my former company leaders.

These wonderful days were overshadowed by the news of the unexpected death of my dear mother. Unfortunately, due to a holiday ban, I was not even able to attend the funeral. This also meant that the only opportunity to meet my four brothers, who were all in the field, back home was lost. Even my brother Hans, who was with the air force in Romania, would have made the trip possible.

The long winter evenings in the confined space of the position went by slowly. Then, in early spring, I had the good fortune to spend a few days' holiday at home. The desolate emptiness of my father's house depressed me greatly. My engagement and the resulting second home in Neuwied compensated for this.

After my return to the Eastern Front, the rumours about our planned relocation to the West became more and more intense.

With the violent actions on the western theatre of war and the associated wearing down of large parts of these battle-hardened troops, the possibility could not be dismissed. Our increasing assiduity in close combat drill also suggested an imminent deployment in western combat gear.

Illustration 3: Author in Russia

Illustration 4:April 1916 Dünaburg; medical visit Sep 1916

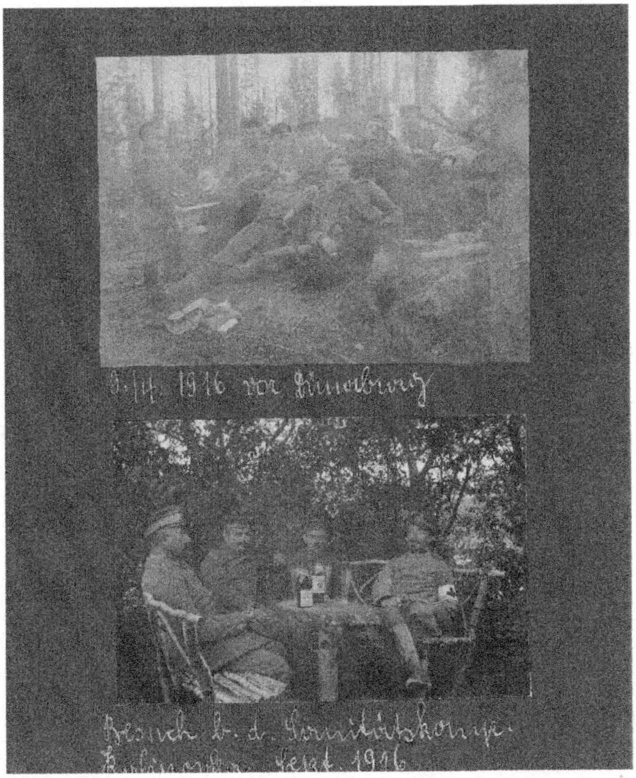

Illustration 5: Dünaburg May 1916 and Easter Breakfast 1916

Illustration 6: Dünaburg Christmas 1916 and Oct 1916

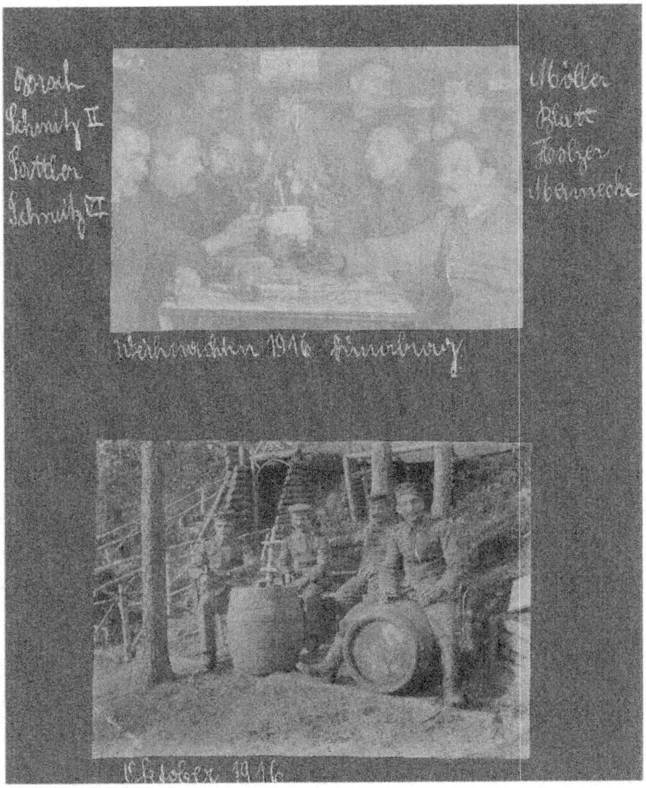

12.Capture of Riga

Meanwhile, we were still in front of Dünaburg, not a foot of ground to spare and armed to the teeth. We had built up this position into a particularly strong position.

The Russians did not begrudge us this fortress, which we had christened Lowzen. The sight of it was unpleasant to them and the greetings that came from it were even more unpleasant. But the Lowzen was not to be taken spuriously either. So they simply wanted to make it disappear from the scene. So they drilled into the mountain. We also let them drill and dig quietly for a few days. Then we got fed up and decided to smoke out the voles. Artillery and sapper officers pledged their cooperation. The day and the nature of the action was decided. The assault squad of our company was drilled. Its leader was Sergeant Hau, as he had been many times before. The start was to be at 6 a.m. sharp. During the night, alleys were cut in the extensive wire entanglement. Shortly before 6 a.m., the sappers had arrived with their explosive material and kick mines and were standing in the trench with the 2 groups of infantrymen. A telephone operator had also joined the strikers. It was little tender Blum. For the first time he was to become active. The last few minutes of preparation were spent in feverish excitement, then it was time to "get everything ready" and the grey figures were already climbing the small storm ladders on the trench wall. Attention: 1 minute, 30 seconds, 10 seconds, one, two, three. Away the brave crowd plodded and squeezed their way through the wire alleys. Soon the first of them had reached the Russian gap. The three guards had not yet grasped the situation in their half-sleep when the Germans were already at their throats. Nevertheless, one of them managed to escape. Then the Russians began to defend themselves, even before the sappers had reached the hill. But now the Russians' bullets were already whistling. The telephone operator fell by the wayside. He no longer answered his telephone. I crawled cautiously out of the trench, crawled through the wire and then dashed in 2 jumps into the extension-trench. The infantrymen had already advanced through the trench, which ran in zigzags, towards the Russian main position. The sappers hurriedly prepared the anti-personnel mines and sealed off the trench to us. On my way back I immediately grabbed the telephone operator Blum. He had been shot in the hip and was screaming miserably. When I put him down just before our ditch, he was shot in the thigh. But we soon managed to squeeze him through the wire. The infantrymen now worked their way back under the protection of our artillery, which covered the main Russian trench. Of the sappers who finally found their way back, one remained behind, dead. He could not be recovered. Two infantrymen were still slightly wounded. Now we were waiting for the reoccupation of the Russian section and the trench, which was so beautifully lined with anti-personnel mines. In our minds we could already see the Russians flying into the air and hanging from the stumps of the pines. Yes, disk blue[9]! The Russians weren't so stupid as to run straight into their trench. It took a long time, then they carefully worked their way up to their positions, threw numerous hand grenades into the trench and thus detonated the mines. Their sappers had been blown up by the sappers during the retreat. The Russians, however, stopped their drilling attempts for the purpose of blasting. It had become too uncomfortable for them after all.

The first revolution had already revealed the impotence of the Russians. The fraternisation scenes around Easter time led to the conclusion that Russian resistance was over. Then Kerensky, the Russian Menshevik[10], gradually regained the upper hand and once again raised a tight regiment.

With enormous means, he attempted one last massive operation in the summer to demonstrate doctrinaire red power.

From 18 to 25 July 1917, the defensive battle at Dünaburg thundered, eclipsing everything we had experienced here so far. The barrage of all calibres lasted three days. Nevertheless, not a single dugout had fallen victim to the twenty thousand shells. It therefore

---

[9] Original German "Ja Schiebe blau: - literal translation. Meaning of the saying cannot be determined.

[10] Member of a minority opportunist group of the Russian Social Democratic Workers' Party, whose policies were directed against the revolutionary program of the Bolsheviks

seemed incredible to us that an attack would be attempted on a broad front. Exactly as had been reported to us from the fighting in Imorgon to the south, the Russians arrived in bright heaps on the morning of the fourth day.

The ravines and slopes again echoed with a terrible roar as our defences came in so unexpectedly strong and with all means at their disposal.

But ever new lines of fire rolled over the hills and blazed at us. Again and again the boldest attempts failed. Clattering and rattling and hissing, it drove into the earth-grey crowds that no longer knew how to get in or out. Dust and smoke and sulphur gases made the horrible picture misty and prevented total destruction.

Our advanced mountain position, an exemplary fortification in which I was staying, came into the possession of the enemy for hours and only through the daring efforts of an officer of the 12th Company with courageous men was our capture prevented.

It was not until the afternoon that the infernal noise died down. Now the battlefield could be seen more clearly. The Russians had left more than 5,000 dead in front of our battalion section.

But we also had many casualties.

A truce of 2 hours gave the Russians the opportunity to bury their countless corpses. The following day, we lowered about 50 dead into the grave in our quiet forest cemetery. These days had cost us more lives than all our previous losses in the 1- and 1/2-year war of position.

The position was once again completely in our possession. But it was so mashed that a transfer was considered.

Only now were we pulled out of the front for the first time and relieved in smaller periods.

The resting position was near Matweikischki. The dugouts were built on top of each other in terraces on steep forest slopes and connected to each other by truncheon stairs. The dugouts had the funniest names.

I was sick for several weeks because I had swallowed some gas and I took good care of myself here. It was a lively life, in which the new replacements, who were now coming, gladly joined in.

At the end of August, our hour also struck here too. After the Russians had annoyed us in July, we wanted to show them how an offensive should be done.

Everything was prepared for the capture of Riga.

After the regiment had been assembled at Josephovo and had spent a comfortable day of rest, we went to Abeli station where we were loaded.

We hadn't experienced anything like this for years, and we involuntarily thought that Riga might turn into a "West" after all. But that was not the case. The journey did not go far either. In Raziwilischki we were already put out to air.

We had to share our night quarters with Russian prisoners who were housed in extensive wooden barracks in the forest.

On 1 September 1917, our advance to Riga began. The outfit reminded us vividly of the days of 1915, when we began the battle for Dünaburg in a large unit.

We were convinced that the road to Riga would be a tough nut to crack. After all, we first had to cross the wide Düna river. It is still a mystery to me today how we managed to do that. After all, the Düna in this area is at least as wide as the Rhine near Bonn.

Whether it is true that the gas shelling, against which the Russians were not yet carefully protected, had a facilitating effect here, I have not been able to ascertain. However, the construction of the bridge must have been a masterpiece of German pioneering work.

At the burning Uxküll we crossed the Düna. About 500 m before the river, we left the protective coniferous forest. We did not engage in any serious fighting. On the first day, we crossed the kilometre mark we had set for ourselves.

It was a beautiful, fertile country that we roamed through. The estates were exemplary by Russian standards. The settlements of the small farmers were also in good condition.

The roads behind the Russian front, where we were now, gave us no cause for complaint. German and Austrian prisoners of war had covered the roads with wooden planks for miles, allowing them to be used in all weathers.

In the pouring rain we reached a tiny village in the evening, where we found accommodation. By the time we had dried our hunks to some extent at the open fires, we would be in good spirits again. The night was extremely quiet in our section. Only from afar did the thunder of guns rumble.

Had the Germans already entered Riga? We did not know. The following day we advanced a little further and arrived in the afternoon at an estate of average size and quality.

We stayed here for five days. We were in good hands with the people. They gave us what was in the barn and the chimney. The enormous supplies we captured in the sudden advance, plus the produce of the blessed land, enabled us to refresh old habits from 1915. All manner of cooking and roasting began again. Cattle, which the fled inhabitants had abandoned, we found tied up in the stables.

The estate people also knew a little German. The masters had fled. The

Hausmannsfrau, as the wife of the master servant was called, met me a lot in the kitchen. The incessant frying of chops caused her to tap me on the shoulder one day and say, "German soldier no good!" I smiled and asked Mattka (that's what we called the older women): "Well, what's wrong with me, mother?" and she reproachfully told me: "Yes, no good, too much food," because she was under the excusable misapprehension that I would eat all the chops myself. That was nonsense, of course. We had introduced a division of labour. One cooked the soup, the other the potatoes and others had done the preparatory work or were out on an "errand". I thought it was necessary to give Mattka, who had brought back some knowledge of the German language from her stay as a seasonal worker on an East Prussian estate, as well as many material possessions, an explanation. I could not bear the insult of immodesty. We then got along well again. In the evenings we sat together with the estate people and made our jokes.

Since we had also received rum because of the bad weather and the Russians also had a taste of it, the mood could easily be raised to the highest pitch.

I had the opportunity to go to Riga by car on one of these days and found a surprisingly beautiful city with an unmistakably German character. The war had done nothing to it. There was, of course, still a flurry of activity in this recently occupied city. The shops still had considerable stocks of goods.

Since I wanted to be back at the estate before dark, I unfortunately did not stay very long in Riga.

We left the manor in pouring rain. We could not imagine why we should march in this cold rain, since Riga, as I had noticed, was in our hands. We therefore did not hold back in our praise of the army command for this dreadful imposition. We had to march the whole day and crossed the Düna again.

What was the running actually supposed to mean? No one knew. We arrived at a forest camp late in the afternoon, soaking wet. The big shelters were not watertight. It was raining everywhere. We had just remedied this with great effort and skill, using the most modest means, when we had to leave again and soon found ourselves at a railway station where we were loaded.

The journey continued to Dauzerons in the area of Jakobstadt. Here we again took up rest in a forest camp for 2 days.

Now the battle for Jakobstadt began.

On the evening of 23 September 1917, we set out in the direction of Jakobstadt. We spent the night in the open not far from the German position. For this weather, camping near Mother Green was an unpleasant event.

On 24 September 1917, Bavarian troops opened the attack. Artillery activity was enormous on both sides. However, the Bavarians captured the enemy position in a few hours.

Endless columns of prisoners met us on the approach.

The bad weather made our progress difficult because no gun could follow in the soggy ground.

We encountered little resistance as we rolled up the position.

We spent the night in barns, some of whose thatched roofs were badly damaged. On the morning of September 25, the weather was a little better and we advanced further. Suddenly, emerging from a forest of firs, we saw the town of Jakobstadt in front of us.

This town was formed by an elongated row of houses running parallel to the Düna River, with only a few small street heads. Near the wooden bridge spanning the Düna, the houses were a little closer together. So it was already a kind of town.

Cautious action in a thin line of firing prevented greater losses in the fire that now began. It was a strange feeling that came over me when I moved against this "town" with the first line of riflemen using the ditch as cover. In the meantime, the place had almost been cleared of the enemy. The enemy had retreated across the river the day before and set fire to the wooden bridge. It was still smouldering. Remnants of the former garrison were still defending the group of houses not far from the bridge. In the process, the artillery on the other side of the river gave them noticeable support. The battle lasted only a short time, then Jakobstadt was defeated.

We held the houses of the southern exit of Jakobstadt.

However, we had to spend most of the time in the cellar because the shelling was very intense. There we were in Jakobstadt without even the smallest cannon.

During the night we received reinforcements. Brave militia[11] soldiers were to occupy, expand and hold the new positions. Thus Jakobstadt, a bridgehead which had hitherto been held by the Russians in many storms, fell in an easy stroke.

After spending the following day and night in Jakobstadt as well, we left before daybreak.

Again we had bad weather and had to build billet roads to get the vehicles with the combat baggage through the mud. The relatively short distance we had to march took almost the whole day. Our night's lodging was in a pub, a small tavern like those that are sometimes lonely at road junctions.

---

[11] "Landeswehr" in German;

In the meantime, we had become army reserves and were taking up rest positions in an abandoned German artillery camp.

To make sure that it didn't get too quiet in the resting position, a strict labour service began. Roads had to be built, bridges and railway subways had to be repaired, accommodation had to be improved and other outdoor work, which was less pleasant for the advanced season, had to be done. October days were sometimes quite inhospitable.

We countered the shortage of food that now set in with self-help measures in terms of food procurement. The lakes gave us fish and hunting events brought us numerous hares and rabbits. We caught the fish with hand grenades, which were available to us in heaps in the former Russian position. We shot at hares with carbines and rifles. We made the ammunition ourselves. The bullet from the infantry projectile was extracted. Half of the powder charge also came out, then some paper onto the part of the powder remaining in the case and shot pellets were poured on top. This work of art was sealed with a paper stopper and the cartridge was finished. Where all the pellets came from, I don't know. I do know that there were several clean farms in the vicinity. It is therefore reasonable to assume that the lords of the manor had left hunting equipment and ammunition behind and that our boys had then found them.

It was also here that I found parts of modern agricultural machinery from Schütte-Lanz in a burnt-down outwork. A sign that our good German goods were also in demand in Russia, if the proximity to the city allowed the profitability of modern large-scale agricultural enterprises.

One day, while we were fishing, which is not without danger, a mishap happened to me that could easily have had nasty consequences. Our beautiful raft - a barn door - had been towed away from the lake. We therefore tried to throw hand grenades as far as possible into the lake from the shore. The things had to be dropped as quickly as possible after they were pulled off, so that they would only explode deep in the lake. The force of the detonation caused something in the belly of the fish to burst. Then the animals came to the surface with their bright bellies. I think this was a fishing practice called overexploitation, which is why a ban was soon imposed. Among us was a young man who was a bit delicate and didn't develop the right momentum when casting. I wanted to show him a feat of throwing, but spat so hard into my hand that the hand grenade slipped from my grasp as I lunged. The reeds on the bank now contained the grenade, which, if not found immediately, was bound to explode in our immediate neighbourhood. And so it did. But instead of searching for the projectile for a long time, I immediately yelled: "Lie down!" The fact that we were now all lying on the ground prevented our injury. Despite this incident, we didn't go back to our camp until we had filled our sandbag to the top with fish.

I often visited the abandoned Russian position. There was so much to sniff out. But it was also equipped with all the refinements. There was even a lighting system for the forecourt, made of pans filled with tar. The roofing of the trench was a matter of course, as I already knew from the field positions of the 1915 advance. The Russians' versatile alarm devices were also quite resourceful. The dugouts of the crews, on the other hand, were small and very low. They could in no way bear comparison with our flats. I found a lot of letters, maps and photos in the Russian dugouts that caught my interest. I couldn't read all the stuff scribbled together in strange letters.

Our resting place did not seem to be a suitable place to stay for the coming winter, so we moved to Mitau, a larger town (by Russian standards) south of Riga.

I stayed here with two very old ladies, the Baronesses von Hahn and von Bähr. After a hard day's work, we spent some very pleasant hours in the evening. We also had the opportunity to visit the theatre. The frozen river Aa was an excellent ice rink. I eagerly pursued winter sports. Fireworks and musical events on the ice rink made this beautiful sport especially desirable to us. The cross-country exercises in the snow-covered landscape were also nice to keep our bones from hibernating. Since the town was inhabited by civilians with whom we had friendly relations, we got to know a piece of German-Russian nationality in this environment. There were few difficulties in communicating because the population spoke more or less good German. It is understandable that we celebrated Christmas particularly well here, because we lived here almost like at home.

13. Napoleonic Winter Campaign Lievland

Around 10 February 1918, I was lucky enough to enjoy another home leave. A railway blockage extended this leave to 4 weeks.

Somewhat weaned on the laudable military activities, I returned to Mitau at the beginning of March.

But in the meantime my regiment had left for Riga. The old Baroness von Helm now told me that a German enterprise against the Bolsheviks was planned in Lievland, today's Estonia. She let slip the assumption expressed by my comrades that I would now be pushed off from the troop assembly point to the Western Front.

Those were "lovely" prospects.

I didn't even think about reporting to the commandant's office but had a good night's sleep and worked out a plan for how I could get to Riga most inconspicuously. When I left, the baroness slipped me a letter to relatives in Dorpat, because she thought I might by chance reach that town in Lievland on my journey. Although I doubted whether I would ever be able to deliver the letter to that address, I took it with me anyway. Then I tried to get to Riga by train. I had no difficulties either. The regiment had already left Riga in the meantime. I also managed to get from the German station to the so-called Russian station in Riga.

But that was more difficult. That same night I boarded the Russian train with its clumsy carriages on supernormal gauge tracks and arrived after about 1 1/2 hours at the terminus of the railway line used by the Germans.

Here I waited until morning and asked the gendarmerie about the deployment plan and marked the deployment route of my division on the map.

A large number of comrades had gathered in this little godforsaken nest. But I found no one who was willing to go with me on the same day. Since I was eager to join my regiment as soon as possible, I set off on my own. Meanwhile, the luggage was weighing me down. I had brought all sorts of useful things from home.

A small sledge was attached to the window of the last house in the village. This sledge could have been a nice way to transport my luggage. So I decided to commandeer it and crept up to the house. It was inhabited by soldiers. Unnoticed by them, I managed to untie the sledge and take it with me.

So I set off on my lonely way to the army road. Uphill I put my luggage on the vehicle and downhill I put myself on it. I reached the road at 2 o'clock in the afternoon and soon found my regiment and the company.

What a surprise for my comrades! I was glad to be "at home" again and felt safe. I had been a bit despondent on the lonely journey with my child sledge through the great white loneliness. I hadn't imagined the distance to be so great from the map.

It was a desolate area that we had to roam through. The road was impassable in many places due to blasting. The bridges had been burnt. No wonder our progress was slow. I had never seen such a strange army platoon in the whole war. Each group (non-commissioned officer and 8 men) had built a large sledge out of slats and boards, which held the luggage of these 9 men. This monster of a sledge was pushed in turn by 4 men. Imagine a regiment of 2000 men on the march like that.

This new marching disorder seemed to me to be the purest Napoleonic winter campaign. But I have to say that this new attempt at troop movement worked out well.

The first night we slept in a Russian position that had been abandoned months ago. The dugouts were not tight. The water that had penetrated was frozen. On the ice sole of these cold dugouts we made a layer. We slept quite well.

The following day we reached Vollmar at a relatively fast pace. From here we used the railway track as a road. The high snow on the railway embankment was made into an ice rink by the groups in front, trampling with difficulty.

The next larger place we touched was Wenden. We only noticed a hint of the enemy. Here half a dozen Bolsheviks were hanging from the telegraph poles. They were in civilian clothes.

Strangely enough, we found the villages only slightly destroyed.

The Bolsheviks had gotten out of the habit of burning. Possibly they thought our advance was only a temporary phenomenon.

From Wenden, the nightly accommodation on the march to Walk, a rather important place the Russians proudly called "town", was already more difficult. There were only a few small farmsteads available, and they were scattered far and wide.

From Walk, where we spent one night, we were more comfortable. The mayor had to make sure that 1000 horse-drawn sleighs were ready for us the next morning. The brave man promptly carried out the order.

Two men were packed into each of these small panjes sledges. The drivers were Russians, old and young. What a ride that was! We were colder than on the walk, but it was still beautiful. The grey chain of sleighs snaked through the vast snowy landscape. It only broke off when the path led over a height. But once you had reached the top of the hill, a new, magnificent picture presented itself. Hour after hour, the good little Panje horses flitted over the snow with their tireless legs. The swirling snow was driven by the wind against the stoic carter, who was dressed in a millennium-old fur coat and behind whom I was hiding. I sat alone in my sledge. Woe betide me when I had to bring an order to the front along this endless line. Then we went at a pig's gallop through the high snow to the side of the caravan.

Our main food was black pea soup with horse meat. Feeding was sometimes three times a day. It was self-evident that the black peas could not be cooked. The morning diet was impeccable because the night allowed time for the pulses to soak. But it didn't matter if the peas were still hard as stones. The hot broth warmed us up pleasantly. The clickers were simply spat out again like cherry stones.

We had to be extraordinarily hasty when taking our food, otherwise the grim cold would turn the delicious meal into a black-brown lump again.

At 4 - 4.50 in the afternoon, quarters had to be found for man and beast. That was a job that fell to me. Once I had managed to get everything settled late in the evening, I fell into the straw, dead tired, to be up early again. After all, in the morning it was necessary to bring the people scattered on many homesteads back to the march road at the right time.

This unique wintry advance, full of hardship and romance, came to an end at Karlsberg Castle about 40 km from Dorpat.

Here the civilians were sent back with their sledges. It was not difficult for them to say goodbye to us.

Karlsberg was a beautiful manor house. The Bolsheviks had left the castle pretty filthy, so we had to do a lot of housekeeping. The administrator of the castle and some of the staff were still there when we arrived and stayed for the few days we were in the castle.

For this building, which by the way was still new, one could really say castle. It was a large, smooth building made of reddish sandstone. The furnishings were simple but tasteful. The room walls were wood-panelled, the ceilings of glazed walnut. The kitchen resembled a modern hotel kitchen. 11 000 acres of land belonged to this manor.

The area here was decidedly more charming than at Wenden and Walk.

Not far from Karlsberg Castle, idyllically situated in a river valley, was a bathing resort. The small, cute wooden cottages were only used by the people of Dorpat in summer. People called these little houses "dachas".

I would have liked to go to the university town of Dorpat because I wanted to deliver Baroness von Halm's letter. So I was very happy when the company leader gave me a lift in his sledge one day. The city of Dorpat has a very different face from Riga. I was therefore somewhat disappointed when, after a long journey, I finally saw the unattractive city with its snow-covered roofs lying in front of us. I didn't see much of the city that day. No other city in the East has ever looked so Russian to me. Since no one took care of the horses for me, I didn't have much time to visit the city. I was not able to deliver my letter on this occasion.

In a few days, however, we occupied Dorpat, or Jurgew as the Russians called it. Today, by the way, it is called Tartü.

I then made up for what I had missed. It was a splendid entry we made into Dorpat. The inhabitants, who had been liberated from the Bolsheviks, left nothing to be desired. I took up quarters with the Baron von Koschkul, who ran a large house. However, the gentlemen did not take much notice of me.

After a few days, I moved in with a German family from Simon.

The occupying forces had taken over the administration of the country. They made use of the existing civilian staff still sitting in the offices and limited themselves to control for the time being. It soon became apparent, however, that the introduction of German administrative methods was necessary in order to create even approximate order and an overview.

The frontline troops, however, were rather poor in soldiers who were up to such demands. It was thanks to this circumstance that I was transferred to the General Command in a few days and had to do duty in the district headquarters.

The offices were located in a former Russian customs building. A huge amount of work awaited me here. The entire German staff consisted of 1 captain, 1 lieutenant and 3 men. Our administrative district was almost as large as the Rhine Province. The population was about 250,000 souls.

The jurisdiction for our work was not exactly defined. Therefore, there was always some friction with the commandant's office, whose field of work was supposed to be limited to purely military matters. The different views on responsibility were understandable when one considers that our powers were delegated by the army high command, i.e. came from a military authority, just as the commandant's offices arose from military necessities and consequently had to be bound by military orders.

In Courland, the situation was of course much clearer and tested in practice due to the appointment of a governor.

Here in Lievland we were not the conquerors, but a police force. So, in a way, we helped the liberated population to regulate their administrative affairs.

After initial difficulties, we worked tirelessly to get the administration flowing. In this, the German intelligentsia among the inhabitants was a particularly tangible support.

The administrative district soon proved to be too large and led to a clean division between town and country.

I, too, joined the newly established town council with a mayor from the Rhineland at its head. In a few weeks, the administration resembled that of a medium-sized German town.

My special field was the tax administration, which was brought up on the basis of the form material obtained from Bonn. The civilian head of the department, which employed about 25 people, was a Baltic-German Baron von Sumson-Himmelsterna.

My regiment had long since left the city of Dorpat and was in Altengrabo to be drilled for use in the West.

Because I now had to have some kind of military home, I joined the 7th Meckl. Dragoons. The Dragoons did not have any particular liking for me. They didn't want to give me a uniform either. I therefore had them bring it to me. The nature of my services and my intercourse with civilians required a corresponding military touch, which had to be expressed in the uniform. I was therefore proposed as a deputy military officer.

The contact with the public led to many invitations to families who were socially distant from me. I spent a particularly large amount of time with the relatives of the Baroness von Halm, where the news I had brought with me from Mitau introduced me warmly.

However, I did not limit the traffic to the German families, as they liked to see. I also liked to visit the Estonians.

This gave me the opportunity to get to know the conditions and concerns as well as the contrasts of the two groups of people we had to deal with in the administration. Hospitality seems to be a general trait in Lievland. After spring had come, the walks on the extensive plateau of the Damberge brought a nice relaxation. The steamboat trips on the Embach, a small river that makes its way through flat, fertile land to Lake Peipus, were also quite interesting. The warm summer evenings brought a lot of people together in the concert gardens of the Warnemine - apparently the Beethoven Hall of Dorpat. Occasionally, I also wandered through the oriental-looking department store in the middle of the city.

Despite my best efforts, however, I was unable to find my way around the Estonian language. This strange language, which has nothing whatsoever to do with Russian, with its full sound of many vowels, kept attracting me.

Once I had to supervise a gathering in a forest for a comrade from the police. I was the only soldier among the huge crowd. At the centre of the open-air event - in any case a kind of May Day celebration - was the speech of an Estonian leader, which ended with the sentence: "Esti, Esti, elagu" - Estonians, Estonians, stick together". What the people were supposed to stick together against, who burst into unending applause at these words, was not quite clear. But they seem to have stuck together very well, because today they are the leaders in their country, whereas before, despite the Russification of the Baltic States, it was the Germans who were the leaders because of their intelligence and culture. I believe, however, that even today the Estonian people give quite a lot of leeway to German concerns.

The hunger for soldiers in the Western theatre of war put an abrupt end to my peaceful work in Torpat.

The so-called Hindenburg Commission arrived in Dorpat one day and was on the lookout for halfway straight bones. The emphasis on my indispensability did not intimidate these gentlemen in the least. "A little bird sang in the wire enclosure: Ka Vau, K.V., K.V." What was the use of all the telephoning, even the S.0.S. call of my city captain was not heard.

PART 3: THE WEST-FRONT

14.France

So at the end of July, I packed my bundle and left. My journey was to go directly to France. In Riga, I interrupted the journey for a few days. So that I couldn't go for a long walk, I was given a command. I had to guard Russian prisoners. In the morning I picked up half a dozen of them at the camp and took them to some administration building to be cleaned. On the very first day a fellow escaped from me. He asked me on the march through the streets of Riga if he could get something in a shop. The shopkeeper was his aunt. Other companions had allowed him to visit from time to time. I did not object to his intention because I felt sorry for the guy. He rewarded my trust with his escape. The camp commander kindly waived my valued cooperation for the rest of the visit.

In any case, the mishap helped to speed up my departure for the West.

On the drive through Germany, I was in two minds for a long time whether I should make a detour to home. Counting off on my buttons prompted me to say "no". But in Bingen I did leave the train and lay down by the Rhine for another hour. I told old Father Rhine all my sorrows and then left for France, a little angry.

One Sunday afternoon I arrived in Thiaucourt, where my regiment lay.

I met only a few old comrades in my company. The storm at La Motte had cost the regiment an awful lot of lives. Twelve officers alone had had to bite the dust in the few foggy hours of the morning of the storm. I couldn't find my way around among the new faces.

The battalion lay in reserve in a forest not far from Thiaucourt. For my eastern view of things, I found incredibly poor quarters in the forest. They did not offer the slightest protection against artillery fire. The company had completely changed in character. Not much of the unsurpassable comradeship was left.

The young replacements who now left their mark on the company did not yet have the esprit de corps that only grows and is strengthened through years of standing together. And this was not what the young people wanted. They had come into the army under completely different conditions and had not remained completely free of the degenerating influence of native criticism.

When I got to know them better, I asked myself whether they could be relied on.

The few days of rest passed quickly. I hadn't quite found my feet when we took up our position. We were near Flirey.

Our opponents were Americans. I was much better satisfied with the position than with the rest camp. Flirey lies in the Priest Forest.

My sphere of action was limited to a grenade launcher battery. The grenade launcher crew consisted almost exclusively of young students. There I had it good and I had to put aside my misgivings. It was a special pleasure for me to get in touch with these bubbly lads.

The area was quite beautiful. We didn't notice anything of the enemy. He was far away from us in the confusing terrain of Flirey.

The undergrowth of the forest, which had been chopped up in 1914, was already growing lush again. Over the deep funnels, benevolent Mother Nature covered a modest sward. Bees buzzed in the modest floral pile of this poor grass cover. For the years of alternating battles that had raged in this region, one would have guessed a more desolate scene. Such near-peaceful conditions I had not expected in the best of circumstances.

I thus had the opportunity to gradually settle in again and felt quite at home in a short time.

Here we were also replaced on a 4 by 4 days.

The resting place deserved its name. The young comrades dragged me along every free minute on their raids to the nearby villages of Bouillonville and Thiaucourt. For the most part, they knew the inhabitants by name and were able to communicate well with them.

Soldiers' homes, cinemas and fuck pubs[12] were also welcome opportunities for us to kill time as restlessly as possible. On the other hand, we sometimes had our retreat days, where we embarrassingly avoided all these more or less banal distractions and lay down in the sunshine in some meadow ground and dealt with all kinds of problems.

Even though we agreed that such hours were better spent than those spent in the scent of gifts, a restless feeling always drove us to put the rough customs of the Landsknechte[13] as compensation against the experiences at the front.

On one of these rest days, we went on an official excursion to a stage village whose name escapes me. Here we got to know a new weapon, the tank. There were several types here that had been taken from the British. We were very interested in these iron elephants. According to the type of armament of these monsters, a distinction was made between female and male tanks. Whether these were really "official" designations, I cannot say with certainty.

When we returned to our quarters from this excursion, I made a bet with a comrade on the way that in the next four weeks we would make

---

[12] Literal translation of "Bumskneipen"

[13] German-speaking mercenaries used in pike and shot formations during the early modern period. Consisting predominantly of pikemen and supporting foot soldiers.

more unpleasant acquaintance with such armoured cars than we did today.

That was around 20 August 1918.

The days crawled along leadenly. The mood at the front was like a typical thunderstorm. The previously usual courageous approach to all the combat activities that the front demanded every day, was no longer perceptible. Yet many visible circumstances indicated that the Americans were up to something.

Their troop movements did not remain hidden. The storage of considerable stocks of ammunition had also become known.

I occasionally saw for myself with a giant telescope that the opposite side was very busy. Wagon after wagon left the fortress of Toul in broad daylight. What would this obvious industriousness have done to our artillery in front of Dünaburg! Here, too, the German aviators succeeded in blowing up an ammunition depot, but the artillery remained silent about all these events that concerned them.

The fact that we were now riddled with trenches on every hill in the vast hinterland did not give me the overwhelming feeling of security that always accompanied me in such situations in Russia.

Only twice had we managed to capture some U.S.A. Army representatives in the battalion area. We were dealing with the division that had received its baptism of fire with devastating severity at Chateau-Thirry.

A major violent reconnaissance by Lieutenant Meng resulted in the complete destruction of an American NCO post.

The airmen came over the front like swarms of locusts. I counted 40 and 50 in one afternoon. Of the tethered balloons hanging in a wide arc around St. Mihiel, one or more were shot down every day. But there must have been a considerable supply of these sausage casings, because there were always replacements quickly.

In order to throw the dice again, our pioneers prepared a gas attack. This devil's dance was of course new to me. I therefore followed the work with eagerness.

What I saw was a small trench, about 30 cm deep, in which bottles of the coal-acid type were posted at small intervals, with a slight inclination towards the enemy. These innumerable bottles were connected by a cable that enabled the simultaneous ignition of the gas containers.

A tedious evening walk to the battalion command post led me past these eerie things. When the wind was favourable, the contents of these thin-walled steel cylinders could eat their way into the bodies of the Americans with insidious treachery. In a sentimental mood, I didn't dare give such a grim mission my evening greetings to the Yankees.

On this evening, the concentrated charge was detonated with one blow on the cue: "The red dog can come". As if by a great flash of lightning, the dramatic stage was illuminated for a moment. Whether the things had their devastating effect is beyond my knowledge.

However, the event was cause enough for the Americans to shower us with a heavy fire assault, which is why I did not return to the company section until after midnight.

The incident was forgiven by the Americans in a few days, judging by the artillery activity.

But it soon turned out that the calm that now came was an eerie calm before the storm.

The Americans had been steadfastly making their preparations for a large-scale action in the St. Mihiel Arc. For once, they wanted to strike a decisive blow against the German front independently of their allies. The English and French, war weary as they were, will have indulged them in the extra tour. The American soldiers did not stand out from among their allies as being particularly fit for war. As newcomers to the world war, they were understandably not yet battle-hardened, but they were inspired by the will to assert the big-man mentality that had been instilled in them. The Americans' arrogance was understandable in view of the enormous enthusiasm they received from their many friends regarding the unlimited possibilities of help.

15. The Americans Are Coming

On 11 August 1918, the Americans had brought their preparations to that level of perfection which must have put the success of the planned offensive beyond doubt.

The mysterious calm was interrupted by the cautious firing of the guns that had been brought into position. Around noon, we were informed of the Americans' intention to attack. Such slogans were always met with suspicion. In this case, the timing was very precise.

Towards evening, we moved into an unfamiliar section of the front in front of Flirey. A pouring rain accompanied us on our march. It rained with persistence even as we struggled to find our way in the filthy trench. The water ran like rivulets gurgling through the trenches and squeaked in our boots. Those who had to run back and forth in the section used the cover, at least there the boots only got dirty, but not so wet. It was impossible to get our bearings in this pitch-dark night.

Catching a well-prepared attack in this shithole, was all that we needed. At the same time, I still had the enviable privilege of being assigned to the forward posts[14]. This consisted of several gunner's nests located in shell holes a few

---

[14] "Schützenschleier"

stone's throw away from the actual gunner's ranks. In quiet times, staying in such nests is bearable because they are less exposed to artillery fire than the recognised fighting trench. In the event of an expected attack, however, one cannot shake off the feeling of being a forsaken man on a lost post.

So it was with mixed feelings that we death-candidates moved to our morass nests. We had small M.G.s and pistols with us.

At 11 a.m. sharp, the Americans opened their destructive fire on our trench.

Right at the beginning, gas grenades were mixed in with the rapid succession of bullets of all calibres. The howling, hissing and crashing of the shells was mixed in ghastly dissonance with the alarm noise of the gas detectors and the S.0.S. shouts. Ga-a-a-a-s Ga-a-a-s! Now we had to hang these choking pots under our snouts as well.

For two hours, which seemed like an eternity to me, I was squatting in the swampy hole with two comrades. The whole howling mess went over our heads. Only a little of it came down in our immediate neighbourhood.

Finally we carefully took off our gas masks. Ah, what a relief! The air "direct from the hand" wasn't nice either, but at least there was enough air. You were in danger of suffocating under the mask.

The rain fell continuously. The drumfire also continued until dawn. And the dawn was terrible. Powder vapour and sulphur were rolled over the ground by the heavy wet air, from us to the Americans. They must have been sweating like us under gas masks, the wind had made sure of that.

At 5 o'clock the tank battle began, hitting our neighbouring Regiment 400 and so much more with tremendous force.

Only 3 tanks limped and rattled ahead of our section. In the dim fog only the outlines could be seen, or more, could be guessed. Slowly we backed away from the monsters into our position. The fire of the American artillery had moved back. Meanwhile, the many sinkholes and the shrubbery prevented the enemy from advancing quickly in front of our position.

However, when our situation here also became untenable, we withdrew to the strong reception position, the so-called Fulda barracks.

Here, when the American attack had come to a halt, we had to endure another barrage. But the bomb-proof shelters gave us sufficient protection and the fighting mood was not bad.

The Americans did not succeed in snatching this position from our hands either. Unfortunately, the fighting in the rear showed us that our neighbouring regiment had long since been overrun.

We no longer had any contact. The company commander had gone to the battalion command post. A single officer was still in the Fulda barracks. If the fire was moved back, we were already at the command posts, throwing hand grenades into the foggy foreland and banging what came out of our rifles.

We couldn't be taken head-on, we knew that. But the enemy also found this out and took advantage of the opportunity offered by the retreat of our neighbours to attack us from the flank and even from the rear. He succeeded in doing so, since we had no support from our artillery. They no longer knew where they were and had to change positions with half their armour. The banging from all sides showed that we were trapped.

Now we were told: The Americans are in the trenches! Back, back! I and 23 comrades managed to force our way out of the Americans' grip.

During our fall back, our lieutenant fell in a trench. One of the dirty 6.5 artillery shells that whistled through the area hit him a few metres behind me and beat him to a pulp.

We came to a road embankment that in a compact mass bisected a small valley basin. This valley, resembling a large bowl, was about 300m in diameter. A deep tunnel had been driven into the embankment, which gave us plenty of space. Right next to the entrance was a shelter. Here we hunkered down and took a breather for a while, for we had hurried here in a fast run.

No one really knew our situation. Everyone had a different view of it. But we were not lost yet. With my loyal friend Will Mennicken, who was in charge of the telephone squad, I agreed to risk a sortie through the barrage. Mennicken was a daring fellow; he had taken the E.K.I[15]. in the fighting at La Motte, which I did not take part in, and was eager to go on leave to marry his Martha, who was urgently awaiting him. For she was no longer waiting for him alone and he wanted to save her from disgrace by marrying her, as he said. The leave slip had already been written when we suddenly had to take up our positions the day before. Mennicken had been through so many times in Russia. So we wanted to put all our eggs in one basket.

None of the others wanted to follow us. But we tried. Twice the fire threw us back. Planes swept so close over us that we could make out the guys' faces, spitting at us with their machine guns. The artillery fire, both German and American, kept pushing us into the embankment.

Then, with heavy hearts, we gave up and crept back into the tunnel to wait for "better weather".

The better weather soon came and with it, countless Americans lining the road embankment and the embankment semicircle. They kept shooting us into the tunnel entrance. We threw out a lot of the hand grenades we had

---

[15] Iron Cross I

here. Now they were also hitting us with hand grenades. They had long-handled baskets with them that were full of hand grenades.

16. Captivity

We were smoked out in our catacomb and had to leave the gallery. The first two people in the passage jumped out. They were a sergeant from the foothills, the length of a tree, and a corporal from East Prussia, also a giant in stature. The Americans stopped. But as more and more people emerged from the tunnels, a few hand grenades were again thrown from the tightly drawn circles of the khaki people. A few shots were also fired from pistols. The tree-length sergeant fell to the ground, struck by a deadly hit. The East Prussian was also shot. A hand grenade sent various splinters into my calves.

Then 5 or 6 officers, including a Frenchman, appeared on the crest of the hollow. The commotion broke up. The officers had shouted for us to be brought up. Now the rest of the tunnel dwellers had come out and we marched single file up the embankment to the officers.

The escort had us stop in front of a cheval de frise[16]. The Frenchman started talking about the officers on the other side of the cheval de frise. He asked for a soldier who could speak French. Comrades pointed to a medic who was from Switzerland and had spoken of knowing French. But no communication was possible. The

[16] "spanischen Reiter" - a defense consisting typically of a timber or an iron barrel covered with projecting spikes and often strung with barbed wire

Americans noticed this and a fat officer, at any rate the devil's chief, asked if anyone knew English. I understood his question but did not answer. Then someone in the group pointed at me and the major, who was the fat man, asked me specifically if I could speak English. When I answered in the affirmative, he had the cheval de frise move aside a little and let me approach. To calm me down, he handed me a cigarette, which a soldier lit for me. The first thing he said to me was this: "*You need not be afraid, for you the war is over. Tell this to the people*". I knew little English and what little I knew was also confused by the extraordinarily exciting situation. However, I had understood the few words spoken slowly and deliberately clearly in their meaning and interpreted them to my comrades as well. Then the fat man asked me where we were coming from: "*Where are you coming from?*" "*Where are you coming from?*" is quite an elastic question and I replied that we had come from that hole. Since he had perceived that himself and wanted to know something else, he was incensed by my answer. He held a map under my nose, but I couldn't read it - after all, I had never been around maps. When I proved too stupid, he pointed to the wreckage of some machine guns and said I could probably handle them better. I felt I had to point out that I had never had anything to do with a machine gun. The Frenchman, at his side, indicated with his riding whip that the interrogation could only produce something fruitful by being suitably forceful. But the American was too decent for that. He explained with a triumphant smile that they had already advanced far beyond Thiaucourt and would be in Metz in three days. Then the staff moved on and left us to the henchmen.

They led us away. There were many of them, a sign that they were still afraid of us. We hadn't gone far when we came across American soldiers struggling with their wounded.

We were now forced to carry the wounded for them. The stretchers, made of canvas and wooden poles inserted into each other, were unsuitable for transport in this rutted terrain.

The two German porters had to pay for every cry of the wounded man they carried with a kick in the butt. I therefore suggested extending the carrying poles with flexible hazelnut sticks so that the bearer would be springy. This innovation, conveyed with more or less skilful use of sign language, met with the approval of the Americans.

They therefore cut off the slender shoots of the nut bushes. I took part in the selection of these sticks and let my small pistol, which I still carried in my pocket, slide into the mud. This took a heavy load off my mind, because if the Americans had found my beautiful pistol from the Dorpat arsenal during the countless body searches I had to endure on that first day of my imprisonment, then woe betide me.

When we were radioed by our own artillery on our march to Flirey, past the advancing artillery and the retreating infantry reserve, we were grateful to them for their transmissions, even though they could be just as dangerous to us as they were to the Americans. But we did have a stinking rage against them because they plundered us. My wedding ring, which I wore on my left hand as a fiancé, was spared from their grasp. My wristwatch, a prize from the Novo-Alexandrovsk fighting games, and a cigarette case, on the other hand, fell victim to the Yankees' addiction to souvenirs.

In the village of Flirey we saw the first coloured Americans. They were not yet considered worthy of front-line combat. Therefore they did labour service and provided the material supplies. They greeted us with loud tumult. Laughter was on their black faces. From their big red mouths under their flattened noses they shouted "*Fritziboy*" at us. At the same time they bared their dazzling white teeth and twisted their eyes with the strange reflecting white. They were all delighted that their white brothers had brought in captive Fritzi's.

I asked my companions on the way if any prisoners had been taken yet. They said no, we were the first. I was terribly annoyed that this misfortune had to happen to me in the fifth year of the war. When we were ordered by officers coming along the way to build roads and had to use sandbags to drag wobbly stones into the tracks of the roads, I already considered fleeing. But the escort was damn vigilant. Escape with success was out of the question.

Around noon we arrived in a village and were led to a large meadow behind a slope.

The place was teeming with German prisoners, and I was speechless at the abundance. It is said that there were over 5,000 of them. After a short rest, during which I was able to see and speak to our severely wounded East Prussian from the tunnel once more, the Americans set us on our march.

The American escort that now accompanied us on our departure was on horseback. It was M.P. (Military Police). They took their job very seriously. If we encountered vehicles or troops on the way, the M.P.s would shout "*Go on to the right*!". That sounded like "So eine Schweinerei![17]". If the evasion did not happen with the desired speed, the "erasers" of the M.P.s flew around our heads.

It was a pitiful train that was on the move. Our boots and clothes were covered all over with dirt. The little bit of sunshine that smiled down pitifully on us around noon and warmed our bodies had dried the dirt to some extent, which made us appear all the more like walking lumps of clay. The non-uniformity of our uniforms, which did not make an excellent impression without a belt and side arms, especially in this state, and the fact that some of us were walking in a coat, others wore a cap and still others had a steel helmet on, and some had to walk bareheaded, prevented us from forming a smart marching column.

---

[17] "Such a mess" – effect is lost in translation. Schweinerei = "piggery"

After this procession, the Americans dragged us through several villages, where we were greeted "warmly" by the civilian population. The welcome was not limited to the sweet words such as: Boche, cochon etc. Sign language was also used and women and men, even children, made the signifying movement with the flat of the hand under the chin. At the same time, the tongue hung out of the mouth as "gracefully" as possible. We let these kindnesses pass us by with an iron face. These expressions probably told the French that their obscenities did not cause a shattering impression. They therefore began to spit and spout and threw stones into our column. As far as this was perceived by the M.P.s, they kept order.

We were always happy when we had such a village behind us and saddened when another one appeared in front of us. We couldn't shake the feeling that the Americans were taking us for a long walk for advertising reasons.

At 5 o'clock we were led to a large meadow surrounded by a barbed wire fence. Here a French officer, whom the Americans had borrowed, had us line up. He spoke fluent German and also scolded us fluently in German. The Alsacers[18] and Poles were segregated from us. The farewell these select people took from us was not very cordial. However, this may have been due in large part to the encouraging remarks shouted at them.

---

[18] Those from the Alsace region.

We were revised more thoroughly here, that is, even more than before was taken away from us. Every sheet of paper, no matter how insignificant, and every picture that even had a word on it was burnt at the stake.

When we were allowed to leave this cattle pasture again after a short time, we were glad, because we thought we would get shelter somewhere. Another three-hour march brought us near a larger town.

It was getting dark and we longed for a camp. After the excitement and frenzy of the day, the tired body claimed its right to sleep, but of all the roofs we saw before us, none was for us. Once again, we were herded into a pasture. The "savage" black soldiers were still hammering the last staples into the 2 1/2 m high stakes that held the barbed wire.

On closer inspection I noticed that this "camp" was divided into several self-contained sections. Our transport filled five such compartments. All 4 corners of the extensive camp had an observation post equipped with a machine gun.

The camp regulations, which were now made known to us, forbade us to do anything that could be forbidden in any way. Lighting a match was then answered with shooting. Of course, escape was punishable by death, and afterwards you would be blackened.

There we were, standing like Oldenburg cattle in the pasture. The night showered us with rain, and it was also very cold. With our empty bellies, we found this particularly hard. We stepped like camels from one leg to the other on the quickly softened meadow floor until we collapsed from tiredness. I didn't even have a coat with me. But the wet ground ensured that we did not stay married for too long.

A night spent like that lasts endlessly. It awakens homesickness and makes one unmistakably aware of the desolation of the helpless situation. As a soldier, one can bear these hardships much better than as a defenceless prisoner.

The next day brought us some sunshine and dried our wet clothes again. Gradually, some small groups formed among the prisoners. They gathered together in order to be able to scold and endure better together. Besides the sunshine, we would have liked to have had a bit of food. We were used to that from home. But that was not yet available. The stones had not yet become bread.

After another night, we got a "ship's biscuit" and a piece of "Wilson bacon" in the morning, moving from one park to the other. We had called it that out of annoyance because it was so flabby and had yellow nests here and there in the flesh. We gnawed on the biscuit like mice. This had to be done speechlessly, because if we spoke or laughed, the gnawed biscuit flour flew out of our mouths like dust.

In the afternoon, the Americans finally tried to give us something to drink. For this purpose, the guards placed horse buckets of water in our camp. But since we had no opportunity to draw water, we fell over the buckets to drink from the hollow of our hands. Our thirst, however, did not show us any kind consideration and we pushed a bit impetuously because everyone wanted to drink something at last. But the Americans were terribly upset by the confusion. They simply knocked the buckets over with their feet and that was the end of the game.

Meals were now served regularly in the morning and evening. The previously given dry rusk was now replaced by the less dry French white bread.

In the afternoon of the 4th day of our stay in the meadow, an American corporal appeared, opened the gate of our camp, and grabbed 5 men for work duty. I was one of the five. We marched behind him to a large tent and had to cut up white bread for the next meal and make cocoa. These were given to the seriously ill comrades who had been kindly accommodated in his tent. We thought it was wrong to go hungry when the barns were full, and on this rare occasion we had a good meal. The Americans didn't bother us at all. They even allowed us to fill our pockets to bursting point after we had finished our work. The supplies captured in this way were distributed to the comrades who had obviously suffered the most from the inclemency of the weather. This was highly appreciated.

In the meantime, a considerable number of cattle cars had been coupled together on the railway embankment, visible from the camp. We could therefore count on an imminent transport.

I wouldn't have objected if I had been on the first transport right away. But I was in camp 3 and if it was to go in order, I would have had to wait. Standing and lying around all night without a coat was almost an abomination to me. But it was also not allowed to go through the wire fence. But after dark I tried and got into camp 1. But first things don't happen, and second things don't happen. The Americans let the last be the first. The next morning, they began the evacuation of Camp 5. So, I thought to myself, we've missed the boat.

But now I didn't want to help fate any-more and saved myself the walk with obstacles to camp 4, which I had envisaged for the second transport.

As luck would have it, however, the Americans took camp 1 away the following day. So, the 6 days of purgatory were over. The luxury train of the Grande Nation, which was waiting for us on the railway embankment, did not easily allow the conclusion that we were leaving purgatory and heading for heaven.

It took an endless amount of time until the khaki men had placed 50 prisoners in front of each of the small cattle cars. But finally the command to "get in" - towards America, one thought - came. We weren't exactly crammed into this small wagon like herrings in the Ronne. But we felt this crampedness more impressively than that because the herrings were dead. We, on the other hand, were still more or less alive.

The food supply, which was set up in two corners of the wagon and consisted of round white bread and tins of canned food, taught us that the journey to America was a long one. It has, to be said, that we were well provided for. The Americans had not been stingy about it. Our farewell went off without a sound. We were not allowed to sing or play the flute.

We were guarded by a white and a black soldier in the car. The clever Americans had worked it out quite sensibly with the two different soldiers. In our opinion, the black soldier also had to have a guard, otherwise he might have eaten us.

He didn't necessarily have to think we were human. According to the names we were given, we could well belong to the animal world.

If we had known how long our rations would last, it would not have been difficult to distribute the noble booty. But the guards made such sinister faces as lion tamers in the circus when they enter the kennel. What would those guys say if one tried to snatch the military secret of our troop movements from them? From such a distance, they must have been able to take a little well-placed speech. But in the end, it was better to remain silent.

The wagon occupants had formed three sections. One section was allowed to lie down, the second was allowed to sit and the third had to stand. By taking turns in this way, the space in the wagon was just about enough.

When one has been driving around for a while and has satisfied the biggest chair[19] by looking out and around, then you think about "taking" and are also inclined to do something daring to satisfy your appetite. This is how I felt when I approached the "white man" to settle the ownership of the food.

He did not know anything about the duration and destination of the trip. We should eat until we were full, he said. When the available "food" had been used up, we could go hungry for a few days if necessary. This primitive interpretation of the food problem, which seemed so complicated to us, was simply classic.

We then proceeded to the sharing. The distribution of bread was not difficult, of course, but those tins with the mysterious labels presented us with certain difficulties. It was a good thing that the canning factories had not only labelled the contents in writing, but also depicted them quite attractively in pictures. At least we knew roughly where we were. But it was still not possible to always meet the individual's taste in the allocation.

I still remember quite well that it came to 2 1/2 loaves of bread and 4 tins per head of the wagon population.

---

[19] As in presidency / chairmanship

So, we could have travelled for a week without feeling too much stomach rumbling.

Our route went via Paris - Orleans to Tours.

We didn't get to see much of Paris. Long before we touched this city, the doors were closed. And that was just as well. At least the stones meant for us stayed out of our car.

I was able to see Orleans in detail. The city made a good impression on me.

Our journey came to an end in Tours. We had been on the road for 30 hours but had often had to lie in wait on the route because other transports were in a greater hurry than we were.

Shortly before Tours, to which we did not have immediate access, some comrades tried to leave the car. They also informed the guard that they had to do something. He let them go. To be polite, they didn't do their business right next to the track but walked a few steps into the field. Suddenly another guard shot at the supposed runaways. Holzer, a medical orderly, received a fatal shot. The poor fellow had fallen victim to the gross negligence of a black American. The corporal of the guards was indeed very displeased with the overly officious black man. But only a few notes were made, the dead man was taken away and, despite our snorting faces, it was business as usual with alacrity.

At Tours station, there were girls on the platform holding refreshments for passing troops.

Some seemed ready to hand out cigarettes to us prisoners. Then a rickety, haggard French stage corporal came sweeping up and forbade the girls to give us anything. Turning to us, he said literally, "No, nix there, you Sweine, if Kaiser kaput, then yes!" Well, we thought sneeringly, now we know where we are again. The Grande Nation had once again sent out a calling card.

With the rest of the bread and cans under our arms, we marched after a while towards a shantytown that had been built before Tours.

But here, too, we didn't get into the barracks for the time being. We walked nicely around them again and ended up in a large, enclosed meadow in our old habit.

Here, after an old American sergeant had "greeted" us in our native language, we had to throw all the bread we had faithfully and obediently brought with us onto a pile to be burned. That's what the old sergeant, who pretended to be Hindenburg, wanted. Then we had to line up alphabetically.

In alphabetical order, we left the meadow in single file and entered the large reception hut. Of course, I, with my "Sh", still had a long time. For the sake of my own satisfaction, I would have liked to be called Abelspiess for a change. But nothing could be done. There was no tinkering here. Only patience: "The soldier waits half his life in vain", as a military saying goes. Time went by on the meadow too, the old, gnarled sergeant from Uncle Tom's hut made sure of that.

Finally, I had "wormed my way" into the reception barracks. But there was something going on in front of it. The Americans seem to be great at "recording".

They had opened a kind of "Conny Island" here. Our personal details were quickly punched into one of the many typewriters operated by Germans, our pay book and money was handed in and packed into a sturdy envelope. The contents were neatly noted on the envelope, just like in a bank. In the next bower we had to strip. Then we went from the scales, past an American military doctor who gave us a cursory examination, to the dressing rooms. When my modest weight was called out to the doctor, he referred to me as a jockey. But in reality, he must have seen me as a horse, because he gave me a gentle blow on the buttocks with his riding whip to signal that the examination was over. It's actually more polite to say goodbye to a jockey with a handshake.

The getting clothed on the run was delectable. To the right and left stood the storekeepers with their clothes. Regardless of your body size, you were given whatever you needed: 2 shirts, 2 pairs of pants, 2 pairs of stockings, 1 pair of shoes, 1 pair of breeches, 1 skirt, 1 pair of wrap gaitors, 1 field cap, 1 straw sack, 2 woollen blankets, 1 towel and a pack sack. Dressed in Adam's costume, all the stuff was received. Once you had passed the long line of issue, you stood outside with your "belly-load", threw all the junk on a pile in front of you and began to cover your nakedness. We quickly jumped into the clothes and then made fun of each other in our new attire. One didn't like this, the other didn't like that. Strangely enough, almost no one could be persuaded to swap. The Americans had dyed the trousers and skirts green and clearly marked them with the sports badge P.W. (Prisoner of War).

No matter how rough and tumble you are, such clothing makes you think. It was not easy to exchange the field-grey uniform I had grown fond of, for these prisoner's clothes.

I felt so sold out. Even the crudest gallows humour could not hide that. After getting into our uniforms, we also received our mess kits and were allowed to stand in line for a hot meal for the first time in 7 days.

The food was good, too good for the long artificial break we had had. We had beans with tinned meat and bacon. I wisely ate only a few spoonfuls of it because I was worried about taking in the overly greasy, hot food after the long dry feeding. So I limited myself to coffee and the nice American white bread.

If you haven't had any hot food for 7 days, you would do well to get used to it slowly on the 8th day. Unfortunately, most of us did not. They feasted as if there was no hot food for another 8 days. The consequences were inevitable, of course.

Our bunkhouses were small. Each 50 men were given one such wooden hut. There were no beds or plank beds in the barracks. We therefore slept on the hard ground.

The present situation, however, meant remarkable progress for us. Wrapped in two blankets, I slept wonderfully. However, the instrumental morning prayer of the guard company, which is obligatory when the star-spangled banner is raised, woke me up at times.

Now I would have liked to have had some water for once to make myself tidy. I didn't want to spit in the air again, run under it and regard this simple process as a morning toilet, as I had to do in the past 8 days.

Getting water, however, was a difficult matter, as the well was not productive enough for this luxury expense. After all, there was an army of an estimated 8 to 10,000 men here behind the barbed wire.

However, I had the idea of going to the infirmary, the precinct room. The reason for this was supposed to be the hand grenade splinters in my calf. They'll have water there too, I thought. I was given a friendly welcome and a little brushing and bandaging. I was also given water to wash my hands and face. However, I had to make do with two drinking cups. If you set yourself up with it, you could do that.

The Americans didn't seem to be in favour of loitering. They put us to work on the very first day. There was an obvious shortage of people who understood English and could speak a little themselves. The Americans therefore grabbed anyone who could even manage a bumpy sentence in English and used them as interpreters.

When we arrived on the second day, a second lieutenant asked those people who could communicate in English to come forward. Because I said to myself, as much as this lieutenant can speak German, you can definitely speak English, I stepped forward with several other comrades. That made me an interpreter. In fact, I knew very little English, having only learned it in passing. I didn't understand the gnawed mutterings in the Americans' gum-chewing mouths at all.

What was there to know? The less one knew to translate, the less was said.

Daily contact with the Yankees soon taught me the most common forms and phrases. At first, like the other interpreters, I was always under pressure and almost longed to be relieved again.

When I voiced my concerns to the Americans, they were quick to respond with the encouraging reply: "You speak verry well". But that was not true. The one who spoke very well was Benjamin the Jew, a foreign traveller who knew his way around half a dozen languages.

We stayed only a few days in Tours, then we (450 men) were assembled as a work company and transferred to the Bordeaux area. Here we arrived early one morning.

Thick fog still hid the face of our new home from us. With the fog, our hopes of a paradise soon vanished. What we saw all around were large wooden houses with corrugated iron roofs. These were not barracks, 108 of these houses measuring 100 x 28m stood here. They also measured 25 m to the gable end.

The 450 men only filled modest corners of such a space.

The Americans called these buildings warehouses.

Our stay was to be only temporary in these mammoth barracks. The camp for us was not quite ready yet.

Our labour service began on the very first day. We had to throw coal onto the locomotive tenders. It was not a good start to our labour service. About 100 men took part in this work at a time; the rest had other occupations. The water shortage, which also existed here, ensured that no one could get past the coal bunker commando. Those involved could be recognised for days to come by their black nostrils and dirty earlobes. With half a drinking cup of water at our disposal for cleaning, the traces of the "moonlighting[20]" could not be completely erased.

---

[20] Original German “Schwarzarbeit” literal translation “black work“ gives context.

It was here that we were allowed to write home the news of our capture on pre-printed postcards.

We were instructed to express our news in the following sentences: "I was captured by the Americans on 12 September 1918 near Thiaucourt and am living in the Bordeaux area. I am doing well. Many greetings to all".

However, my message did not reach home until my relatives had already received knowledge of my fate through the "Red Cross" via Switzerland.

My brother Hans, who was in the air force, was taken prisoner the same week as I was. The French had caught him. Now only one of us five brothers was left at the front. He was with an assault battalion in the West. The eldest brother was missing. The earth had swallowed him up in a big blast in Champagne. Nothing more was ever seen of him. Our youngest had been shot in the knee after a few months at the front and after a year of hospital care had been discharged to the munitions factory in his hometown.

We only had our quarters in the big warehouse for a few days, then our camp was ready, and we moved. The Americans called it move-day.

Our camp was near St. Sulplice on the Gironde.

The necessary wooden buildings were erected around a spacious square. The whole thing was surrounded by a double 3 m high barbed wire fence. The space between the two fences was about 2 1/2 m. To the right of the large entrance gate, which was adorned with a sentry box and headed "Laborcompanie", was the large dining room, the mess hall, with the kitchen. Opposite it was the writing room, the sick room, the workmen's room and the latrine with the washrooms. In the background rose 5 crew barracks, all the same size. I would like to forget the prison in my list of rooms. But that is not possible. This superfluous building stood just to the left of the guardhouse. It had only three cells, naked and bare.

The furnishing of our barracks was militarily simple. Most of the space was taken up by the two-bunk beds made of slats. Space was left in the middle for the stove. There was also a sitting area.

As time went by, we settled in quite comfortably. We still had no straw for our sleeping bags and lay on the cots. But the strenuous activity ensured that we found our sleep even on the hard bed.

17.The Regulated Life

A regular life now began for us.

We woke up at 6 o'clock.

Morning coffee was taken in the mess hall. This first and only breakfast consisted of a soup made of semolina flour, groats or oatmeal, which was somewhat sweetened and tasted very good. This was accompanied by coffee and a 3-5 cm slice of white bread with jam or artificial honey, occasionally also with fat spread.

Then they lined up and marched off to work in different squads. The activities were quite varied.

Lunch was served at 12 o'clock. On weekdays this was a stew, the basis of which was always beans. Beans from the tin can or beans from the sack. The meal was always richly interspersed with meat. And again, 3 species, tinned meat, frozen meat or bacon alternated in order. The portions were small but good. Each meal was accompanied by coffee and a piece of white bread with some topping.

In the evening at 6 o'clock was the main meal. It was also good and had the pleasant quality of being quite varied. Only potatoes were almost never on the menu. We found this strange. But when we occasionally got to know them, we discovered that this fruit was almost inedible here.

It came from Spain and was really too Spanish for us. Rice and Turkish corn tasted better to us.

No food or leftovers were allowed to be brought into the barracks.

The eating utensils were rinsed in hot water containers immediately after the meal.

The Americans strictly adhered to the eight-hour working day.

After dinner, we could spend our free time behind the barbed wire as we pleased.

It was actually planned to employ the prisoners according to their occupation. For this purpose, lists had been drawn up with great diligence. However, this principle could not be implemented.

So it happened that today we were building roads, tomorrow we were laying a new railway track, then we were unloading ships or building harbour facilities. The work in the warehouses was nice and profitable. There was always plenty that “fell” to us.

The guards, who were very strict at first, became more and more accustomed to us and were later quite sociable. The escort company was a kind of wounded company. Most of the people had been to the front themselves and had got the hang of it.

There were many soldiers of German origin among them. Strangely enough, they did not reveal this in the early days, out of consideration for their comrades, in order to spare themselves unpleasantness because of the rumour that they were German-friendly. The officers thought the German-American soldiers were biased and took a sharp aim at them. However, when our cooperation went completely smoothly, they too were less sharp.

Of course, there were also American soldiers of German origin who made no secret of their ancestry from the start. Unfortunately, however, they were not always the best in their treatment. Consideration for their superiors and a strongly developed egocentric spirit must have been a factor in their particular severity.

The area where we were was very beautiful. Especially now, in the late autumn days, the Bordeaux wine country had its special charm through the colouring of the leaves of the seemingly endless vines.

What on the Rhine, Ahr and Moselle is painstakingly pulled up steeply rising mountains, here the plain gave effortlessly and with full hands.

The simple wine farms with their red roofs blended charmingly into the colourful autumn picture of the landscape.

Several thousand acres of vineyards had fallen victim to the Americans' desire to build. Where French grandfathers, fathers and sons had tended the vines year after year, German soldiers were now clearing and levelling with a strong fist.

The French were excellently compensated, but the people's hearts still bled when they saw their life's work being destroyed by us.

It was not the large vineyards that were deprived of their property. Almost without exception, small and smallest economic entities in the wine industry went under and apparently with them the worst competitors of the large enterprises, because these small winegrowers were able to depress prices due to their frugality with modest earnings. At any rate, this was the view of the French concerned.

The work was interesting. The working hours flew by. The most modern technical aids were used. Railways and roads with their associated bridges and subways were built in a mad rush.

No court was set on accuracy. Always ahead, the Americans said. "All is made in hurry" ("everything must be done quickly"). The *Ingeneers*, the name given to the technical staff of the American army, tried again and again to spur us on to American haste. Their cheering words "*come on*", "*mak snell*", "*tout de suite*" will still be in the memory of every comrade of the American prison faculty. But we always kept up our so-called Russian pace, which we had observed everywhere among the Panjes. We approached the unavoidable work with stoic equanimity and embarrassing precision, but we did not allow ourselves to be dictated the pace.

Gradually they got used to our ways and let us do what we wanted and said their "*Allright*" to it. But this universal word of the English language also meant almost everything.

When the postman's whistle blew early in the morning as a wake-up call, our response was: "*Allright*?"

The reply was: "*Allright, got up*? (Up already?).

If the troops were to start marching out, then the top sergeant waved by ripping open the gate: "*Allrigh*t".

The squads were counted accurately: "*One, two, three, a.s.o.*"

If the numbers I called out to the top matched the count, he said, "*Allright*".

If you asked the leader or guard on the way: "We're going again like yesterday, aren't we?", then you were sure to get the answer: "*Allright*".

If you arrived at the work site and the ingeneer didn't show up for a while, the guard would simply say, "*Allright*" to signal that we should sit down.

Punctually, it was time to call it a day. As a sign that it was time to stop work, the ingeneer drew a circle in the air with his index finger and added the word "*Allright*".

After the guard had counted the people and found the number to be correct, he commanded "*Allright*" to signal the departure.

Arriving in front of the camp, we were greeted with the call of the gatekeeper: "*Allright*".

The top sergeant now counted off the squad and granted us entry with the words: "*Allright*". However, this "*Allright*" was sometimes followed by a delicate strip search.

So the "*Allright*" went on and on.

What might not have been "*Allright*" with the Americans? My eager efforts to find out had the result that actually only the abolition of beer in the States and thus also in the army was "*not allright*".

However, the displeasure about this also came out openly. On every locomotive, on every board fence were the four significant words: "No beer, no work!". Even on the soldiers' caps I saw small enamel labels: "No beer, no work".

The eternal counting was also a chapter in itself. If I had received one dollar for every count I was subjected to, the Americans would have had one millionaire more at the end of my captivity and their war chest would have been bankrupt.

In time we also got straw for our sleeping bags and had a decent bed. The gauze wrapped around the frozen meat, after thorough cleaning and bleaching, made it possible to cover the beds in white.

What we didn't get was the reward for our work. But we were compensated with cigarettes and tobacco, even chocolate and drops. Every Saturday afternoon we were maltreated with such things.

There was no communal laundry room. Everyone had to do their own laundry in a tin can. The Americans provided enough soap. The free hours on Saturday afternoons were reserved for this work.

There were countless small fires, which were lit with the wood we picked up on the way. It was unpleasant when the freshly washed laundry was stolen off the line by a lazy person who was too comfortable to do the housemother's work.

The treatment of the sick was of the simplest kind imaginable.

The sick were presented in the morning by some interpreter to the doctor in the camp's central hospital.

The American field doctors and their assistants had a thriving business. Our camp contained a total of 12,000 white and coloured Americans, Indochinese, Spanish civilian labour battalions and prisoners of war. Among this large number of people, there are always a number of sick or morose people who need or want medical help.

There was an eternal wait on this occasion.

Diseases that were not obviously recognisable did not exist for the doctors. Anyone who did not carry his head under his arm and also had a certificate stating that it was really his head was received with suspicion.

The Americans started from the premise that diseases were usually caused by gluttony. The cure was a natural consequence of this premise. What was castor oil with us was laxative salt with the Americans.

On the way to the hospital, the diseases were worked out. Sometimes it turned out that the patients had strangely complicated complaints that could not be interpreted at all. Then the interpreter made up a reasonably reasonable illness for these afflicted people. However, they could not avoid swallowing salt.

The treatment of the lightly ill was continued by our own paramedics. They knew exactly where the shoe pinched.

With the increasing bad weather, which destroyed our boots, the foot patients increased.

Anyone who could stand a quiet day in the camp was given a pair of totally broken boots and presented to the Top[21] in the morning. He was so understanding that he employed this man in the camp.

---

[21] Direct use in German – seemingly slang / description of the camp head.

However, we were not allowed to play this game too well, otherwise we would be summarily chased out with all the broken boots. Here, too, we had to stay in the village.

Such a filthy French winter with 4 months of rain is something of a miserableness. The shoes and clothes that had been soaked through during the day could not be dried in the evening on the one stove that every barrack had, even though it was heated until white-hot. We had to bring the fuel with us from work or pick it up on the way.

Dripping wet, we arrived at our camp at noon and in the evening with a more or less long piece of wood. No sooner had we devoured our meal than we were standing around the glowing stove. One after the other, all the wet rags, from our shoes to our hats, were held up to the stove on a piece of wood.

The drying process took several hours, which we exploited extensively with ranting. In the morning we went back into the clammy lumps and in an hour, we were soaked again.

It went on like this every day for weeks. That's enough to give you moths[22].

After many complaints, we finally got mackintoshes. That helped us a lot. They didn't let any water through.

---

[22] A German colloquial saying.

Now we would have liked to have oil hats, so that the rain could not run down our necks and even further. But that didn't happen so quickly. First a demonstration was necessary. We made our own rain hats to protest against the "dry" Americans. We made them from roofing felt. They were shaped like Chinese hats. It looked funny and the Americans didn't want it. But we kept pointing out the necessity of these rain roofs. Then we also got our oil sou'wester.

But the Americans had something else that we would have liked to have. That was the high rubber “over-boots”. But that cost us a hard "preservation battle". The comrades had to fight this battle in the gravel pit. They fought tenaciously for it and finally refused to work. That's when the captain was called on the scene.

He decided: "Work will continue immediately. I will immediately take steps to ensure that the people get the rubber boots for this work." So back into the mud, the comrades said to themselves, but if the boots are not there tomorrow, they will go on strike again. In the evening there were 50 pairs of rubber boots.

Now you didn't get wet on the outside, but you sweated for hours under the rubber. The work had to be done more slowly.

Those who suffered most from the bad weather, however, were the industrious little Indochinese. Their womanly, scanty clothing and the strange Far Eastern hats gave them little protection. To fight back, they drank a deep dark tea. The tea haulers often passed by our workplace with their covered buckets hanging from a carrying yoke. Always to smile, be that as it may, was probably their motto. We used to tease the friendly little men, and if they occasionally couldn't climb onto the high work train, we would pull them up or throw them up, which they would acknowledge with a shriek. They didn't want to know anything about the Americans. They were too rough for them. But for us they stole everything they could get. One afternoon I was standing on the railway embankment with an American corporal when one of these smiling people came along with his tea buckets. The American blocked his way and made him stop. The Chinese put down his load. When the American lifted the lid of one of the buckets to have a look at the brew, the friendly Chinese man took the ladle and offered the Yankee a sip. This bear driver[23] then took a strong "drink" and squirted the entire contents of his loose mouth into the Chinaman's face. This was the only occasion I ever saw a Chinese man not smiling.

The poor little fellow was affected beyond measure and mortally offended. He eloquently expressed his indignation at the slight. Not understanding "American", he used his strange mother tongue. What might he have been saying with his bubbly "*ching tai tu gan schan ti pönn*" as he venomously moved away with his

---

[23] “Bärentreiber“; word used in German Wehrmacht, for example someone “appointed” to be a trainer for a younger collogue.

burden? To teach him to walk even faster, the American gave him a kick in the butt. Suddenly an officer came along. He hadn't noticed the incident, but the Chinese didn't want to miss the opportunity to complain about the treatment he had received. The buckets were already back on the ground and the Chinese man, with his incomprehensible complaint, was standing in front of the baffled officer. The officer laughed at the poor devil and told him to pass on. What feelings might have moved the representative of the Land of the Rising Sun on the arduous march to his column? How much good merchandise will the grievously offended Chinese have spoiled that day out of resentment? In this and similar ways, the big, naughty American children have sometimes shown their tangible superiority to the small, indefatigable Chinese people.

At the end of October we received the first parcel post. This was a significant affair. In the evening, the numbers of the lucky ones who had received a parcel were read out. But they still had a long way to go before they received their parcel. For the time being, the captain still had it. He wanted to see the gifts of love in the presence of the addressees. That was the rule. There could be pistols and infernal machines in the boxes or bottles with germs.

So we marched individually to the captain's house. Here we were led one by one to the office, where two soldiers opened the parcels or boxes. The things were inspected, felt and admired, and handed over to the person entitled to receive them. Only schnapps was kept back because the Americans demanded that we be "dry" out of sympathy for them.

I also had a small package with me, which was the last to be opened. The captain jokingly told his two soldiers that they wanted to examine it very carefully. Among other things, there were cigarettes in the package, a small packet. The Americans wanted a cigarette from me, and I cut it open with my fingernail and handed it to the captain first. Then he saw the picture of the German crown prince on a rosette on the inside of the lid. I hadn't even seen the picture closely yet. Now he called into the next room to the first lieutenant:

> "*Carpentier*!"
> He replied: "*Sir*".
> "*Please, look here*!".
> Pointing to the little picture, he said:
> "*That is the German Crown Prince, to hell with him!*"

With that he tore off the cover and threw it into the burning fireplace.

He laughed as he did so. He didn't take a cigarette; in any case these had been lying with the picture of the German Crown Prince for too long.

That was the end of the first mail reception.

The rainy season brought a complete change in our internal camp life.

In the good weather of autumn, we mostly frolicked in the courtyard after meals. Here we played all kinds of games and sports: wrestling, punching, running, leapfrogging, boxing, football and other ball games. There was especially a big ball that was always pushed over our heads. It measured at least one metre in diameter. The Americans called it a pushball. We made a lot of jokes with that thing. Then there was also a ball called "plum"; it was a kind of football, but it had the shape of a plum. This ball was kicked like a football, but because of its shape it got into an unpredictable wobbly trajectory, forcing everyone to laugh.

The Americans made it a point to teach us their national ball game, baseball. But we didn't warm up to it very much. The game of baseball is a kind of batting game. What the Uncle Sam people found so extraordinarily appealing about it we have not been able to determine.

Of course, we also had a singing club and an orchestra.

The formation of the first one met with no difficulties. Among 450 men, a few good singers are soon found who can sing a nice little song even without sheet music but putting together an orchestra without having even a single instrument is more complicated.

Despite this, or perhaps because of it, it was made possible.

At first, it was only a bear band with a devil's violin, triangle and similar noisy instruments, and one can say with Wilhelm Busch that this music was really connected with noise. But soon a violin maker among us had finished the instruments for a beautiful string orchestra.

If the bear band had already satisfied the Americans abundantly, the orchestra that had been created out of nothing amazed them in awe.

Now a theatre company tentatively set up and began its activities with simple military tales. Soon, however, it dared to attempt to perform classical plays.

So we had our hands full in our free time and whoever wasn't busy somehow sat down with other comrades to play cards. We didn't have any money. But the players knew how to give their activities an incentive and played for cigarettes.

The thinkers sat quietly in a corner with a critical expression, playing the royal game of chess. They were not disturbed by the banal noise of the skat threshers.

TEIL 4: CEASEFIRE

18.Start of the End

On the Sunday before the Armistice, the Theatre Society performed for the first time in conjunction with the Orchestra Association. It was a resounding success. It was to be followed by other bombing successes as it progressed step by step. The beginning had been made. Now, however, almost all comrades were interested in the camp events, which were supposed to provide us with meaningful Sundays after the dirt and bacon of the week.

The ceasefire came as a complete surprise and hit us unsuspectingly. We didn't know what the situation was like at the front. The American soldiers only told us things. The newspapers we happened to get hold of lied. According to the Americans, Metz had already fallen twenty times. When the sentries started their almost daily howls of victory, accompanied by countless shots, we always said: "Metz must have fallen again today.

Before 11 November, Metz had not fallen for a few days. The Americans were already starting to become uninteresting, when on 11 November we saw a procession from our workplace to the St. Sulpice railway station. It was not yet noon when the villagers in their Sunday best started towards the little station.

We thought to ourselves, what is in the air now? The guards didn't want to know anything either. When our lunch arrived - we had our lunch outdoors - we lit a fire and sat down near it to warm ourselves. Then I heard some torn sentences that the corporal exchanged with the guards. Now the corporal also told me that news of the ceasefire could arrive at any moment.

Just as the outbreak of the war had seemed something incomprehensible to me, so now the end also seemed incomprehensible.

A thousand times we had talked about how, when that day came, when we came to a good end, things would go this way and that. A thousand fantasies had inspired us on this subject. And now, suddenly, in a few minutes, the end would be here.

That was why the many people in festive garb had rushed to the station to receive the news of the ceasefire. Should the end of the wrestling of nations now be a celebration for them. Should we only have thrown deposit after deposit of good and blood into the cruel game and the others now win the prize alone?

I did not know where I stood. I felt a bitter taste on my tongue. I was not in a festive mood.

At 1 o'clock sharp, a lot of noise started. First the people in front of the station shouted and fell into each other's arms, then the Americans started shouting and shooting. All the locomotives wailed with their sirens.

The war is over! The war is over.

The war is over, the soldiers shouted, hugged each other, and did a dance of joy. We were infected by the joy around us and made noise and rejoiced too. Our joy was not as unbridled as that of the Americans. We were not completely happy. Our inhibitions could not be completely removed even by the Americans' assurances: "*You go home now*".

Not much more work was done that afternoon. The time until the return was passed amusingly.

Our way led past the American officers' barracks. The officers stood in the doorways and waved at us in a friendly manner. The news of the armistice seemed to have cheered them up too. As we passed, I heard people shouting from one door to the other: "They're so happy, the prisoners. But they are still a long way from home".

Our barracks were bustling with life. There was eager debate about when we should be sent home. Everyone had their own view, based on the laws of war.

The fact of the ceasefire, however, had no influence on our treatment and employment.

We still went to work in the morning and returned to camp at noon or in the afternoon.

Our companions still had the long cheese knives on their rifles so that no one could harm us.

The Americans also kept quiet about the harsh conditions of the armistice. But one day one of us did catch a newspaper containing an extract from the dictation. We put our heads together in the barracks and bit our lips. It was hair-raising what we were reading. We were aware that the comrades were only allowed to learn this truth drop by drop so as not to become too discouraged. But they didn't want to believe even the drop-by-drop dispensed wisdom, because it was just as hard to believe.

It was hard for us to realise that our homeland was occupied by the enemy and that we remained hostages in the hands of the henchmen.

We were no longer captured soldiers, but slaves to be dealt with as it pleased one.

Now a new, tightly closed front emerged in our ranks. The Americans, French, English and Italians no longer had to bother with the generally applicable rules on the treatment of prisoners of war. The Germans had to hand over the prisoners and that was that. There were no more reprisals.

Might took the place of right.

We had to oppose this power with a united will.

We initiated the efforts on this side with the performance of the play "Wilhelm Tell".

A few weeks were needed to procure material and rehearse the extensive play. Christian, our director, wrote down the roles from memory.

Whatever we could find on the many different work sites that could be used for our purpose had to go with us. And what was not needed? Roofing felt and paint for the scenery, hemp rope for wigs, clothes, weapons, wood in great quantities for carpentry of benches, chairs and whatnot.

Here again it was the gauze cloth wrapped around the frozen meat which, cleaned and dyed, had unlimited uses.

The craft room was filled with artists of all trades.

It was interesting to watch the hairdresser dissect a hemp rope hair by hair and bleach and dye the resulting hair substitute, then fashion it into the most beautiful wig. The tailor made men's and women's clothes. He used everything that did not resist.

The performance was to be preceded by an appropriate piece of music and a prologue. The prologue was written by a comrade. Everything was ready to the last T.

There was an expectant mood in the camp. The Americans were also invited. The mess hall was packed. There were only a few seats.

On a Sunday evening at 7 o'clock sharp, things got lively.

The band opened the round of performances full of atmosphere. The prologue "Deutscher lerne hassen" (German learn to hate) fell on fertile ground with us. But we did not want to hate without further ado. We first wanted to show how little we had in common with barbarians and Huns, as which we were always held.

The Speaker was dazzling. The tailors had put him in a tailcoat made from a dyed woollen blanket. The collar, cuffs and tie were made of paper. In the limelight he looked like a real theatre man.

Then the curtains parted, and the play began.

Christian had reserved the role of Tell for himself. The exact play went like clockwork. The Americans were amazed beyond measure and full of honest admiration. It was almost incomprehensible to them that the prisoners had achieved all this despite their seclusion and without any help. But we were also all proud of our own success.

The spirit that flowed from the performances brought about the unity of the troops that we needed for longer than we had suspected.

In any case, the event had the effect on the Americans that they had to see in us, even more than before, representatives of a people that was permeated by a remarkable culture, which enabled it to show its bold face and its ability even in difficult life situations and had to take an appropriate place in the chain of peoples, despite everything that was there.

19. The Waiting

It is not easy to keep 450 people in a small space together smoothly day after day, month after month and year after year.

Some items of conflict suddenly slam into such clumped-together people who bear their fate heavily. But the Germans are not a mindless herd. They are alive and critical. Their treatment requires prudence and justice.

Our camp leader, a Bavarian sergeant, had the necessary qualities required by his office. He was a simple craftsman with a healthy, uncomplicated mind and a loyal German heart that beat for everyone.

The American captain, however, was also a neat fellow. We had to get along with him, too. That's why violent trials were very rare with us.

The escort company was sent back to America shortly before Christmas however, precisely because they were wounded and sick soldiers.

The farewell was more cordial than we would have been inclined to assume in September when we first met.

With the new company, we had to settle in again. They were recruits who were supposed to have the final drill for the front war in France. Such half-soldiers are not particularly good to deal with. They take everything too scaredy-precise.

A prisoner's life strictly by the book is very disgusting. So these guys still had to learn a lot from us. Some things they didn't learn at all.

Despite the relatively good nutritional condition of the prisoners of war, the effects of the weather tore many a gap in our ranks. Many a coffin-like wooden box was dragged into our camp at night and in the fog, and just as secretly carried out with a sad burden.

Dysentery also crept into our camp and claimed victims after long and painful suffering.

My friend was also afflicted by this insidious disease and threatened to die of it. He had already been separated from his fellow sufferers and was lying in the death chamber. Visiting him was strictly forbidden. Nevertheless, I crept to him because he was asking for me. I also satisfied his craving for food and water. If he was already lost, then he should at least eat and drink to his heart's content once more. For long hours of the night, I held his feverish hands and answered all his confused babbling.

The healthy, bloody young lad mastered the disease. We are still good friends today.

I never attended a funeral. But they are said to have been conducted with the usual military honours.

I only saw the cemetery once. It was in La Basines. There were many a German name on the wooden crosses above unadorned mounds. As an American military chaplain was present at the cemetery, I asked him to take a picture. He did so willingly. He had a few pictures sent to me. They turned out well. I still have one in my possession.

The shigellosis disease did not pass me by either. A malaria-like attack of fever shook me up for days and the night camp, 25 cm above the ground, brought me a kidney ailment from which I will probably never be completely cured.

The days and weeks in the hospital were endurable. Here, black and white Americans, Chinese and Spaniards lay together with us Germans in perfect harmony. The food and care, however, fell far short of what our own paramedics offered us at the station.

As soon as I was able to do so, I went out with the Americans in the evening to drink Rotspon[24] in the village. "Red wine is one of the best gifts for old boys"[25]. In the pubs there was always a row with the French, who, discharged from the military, were now looking to reconnect with the girls conquered by the Americans.

On my khaki suit, which I had long since lost, the sports badge (P.W.) was applied with toothpaste so that I could remove it once in a while. So, I didn't stand out among the Americans and had just as much chance with the girls as they

---

[24] Red barrel wine

[25] „Rotwein ist für alte Knaben, eine von den besten Gaben“ – a Wilhelm Busch saying

did. It even happened that I was the cock of the walk. But then the Americans let the cat out of the bag and revealed that I was a German. When I didn't deny it either, the girls visibly backed away from me.

Anyone caught twice leaving the hospital at night was given a clean bill of health and deported.

That's what happened to me.

What else should I do in this Babylon. I can also take quinine in the camp. I was more at home there than in this mishmash of people.

It was also getting close to Christmas, so you had to be with friends.

How were we supposed to celebrate Christmas behind the barbed wire?

Who would have thought in 1914, when we celebrated the first Christmas in enemy territory in St. Marie a Py, that I would experience Christmas in captivity in 1918? And yet this celebration did not take a back seat to the 4 previous ones.

Obtaining the fir trees, without which a German cannot celebrate Christmas, was difficult. There were no fir trees in our neighbourhood.

The cars had to travel far into the country before they could load the coveted trees.

However, the escort company did not spare this effort and got us some trees. The largest of them was placed in the middle of the courtyard. It was lit electrically.

The mess hall and each bunkhouse had a tree that shone in the decorations we were used to.

What the Americans could not give us in the way of Christmas tree decorations, we made ourselves. We had to do without Christmas weather. There is no ice or snow in Bordeaux. But we had all the more rain.

On Christmas Eve, we were still busy on the railway until 4 o'clock, just like on a normal working day. For example, I tightened the screws on the rail lugs with a heavy iron spanner. My friend Rolf had a thick sledgehammer and knocked furiously against the iron rails. It was cold and wet. The cold forced us to grip. Not one minute earlier we were allowed to finish.

We were therefore able to start our Christmas party relatively late.

At 6 o'clock the tree in the courtyard was lit. Instead of snow, cold rain trickled through its branches decorated with colourful light bulbs.

The Mess Hall was decorated for Christmas after the dinner.

The celebration opened with the joyful biblical message. This was followed by the heartfelt carol, "Silent Night, Holy Night", which we have been used to singing since childhood. The festive speech that followed emphasised the special character of our celebration in the prison camp and jumped over to a dialogue with the dear ones who were now also gathered around the Christmas tree in the wide German homeland and whose thoughts crossed with ours.

Then it was on to the gift table. Just as the American soldier received a Christmas package one after the other, we prisoners of the U.S.A. Army received the same. "From your folks at home" was the common sender's name here. The German Army had a Christmas parcel sent to us by the "Spanish Red Cross". In addition, there were the personal gifts and wishes of our loved ones. Although these had arrived earlier, they were only opened now.

We sat together for a long time and talked about home and the Christmas we had experienced in enemy territory. A comrade gave us a harrowing account of a Christmas in Russian captivity in Samarkand.

Deep into the night, this celebration still had its reverberations in the barracks. Many a homesick heart will have tossed its feverish body restlessly back and forth in simple camps, and many a twitching mouth will have sought the pillow to cling to, so that no one should hear the sobbing. And yet the mothers and wives and children far away in the German homeland heard it. Even if the distance from heart to heart was 1000 km, in such matters thoughts and feelings are found that strive towards each other.

The Americans do not know any long and haunting celebrations. It does not fit into their busy rush. Only one Christmas Day is celebrated.

The second day is again grey and sober. Everything goes its usual way again.

The new year also began with rain and work.

We certainly did not intend to remain in captivity for the whole year. The news that came to us was very different with regard to our return home. Today it was favourable and tomorrow unfavourable. Even now we received German newspapers without any problems, which here and there contained a more or less official reference to our fate. Public opinion towards us was ambivalent. This can be said of the official bodies of the time as well as of private opinion in Germany, as far as it was disseminated in the press. For some we were too Bolshevik, for others too national. Each opinion drew its own conclusions for the treatment of the prisoner-of-war question. We had to watch this useless battle of opinions of those home.

This realisation and our own impatience forced upon us the view from behind the barbed wire that the homeland had enough to do with the demobilised troops than to look forward to our accelerated return.

If only this dirty winter was over again. Spring was a better time to hope and wait.

Fortunately, our work on roads and railways decreased. The warehouse work in the big department stores was a more bearable occupation because it was done under cover. But here, too, the work was very different and depended in its pleasantness on the storekeeper and the posts. Preference was given to work in the food and clothing barracks. Depending on how the search went, we helped ourselves to the best we could from the immense supplies, so that at lunchtime and in the evening, we regarded the camp kitchen as an unnecessary, even intrusive, institution. In addition, however, a decent supply of cigarettes was also provided. Home-rolled cigarettes, which delighted us in the early days of our imprisonment, we now found unsuitable for labouring prisoners and rejected them. We took the ample opportunities offered for our "errands" and served the timid guards to boot.

I got fed up with this drip-feed one day and once provided a whole month's supply in one fell swoop.

I had discovered cigarettes, brand "Mogul", a good variety in cardboard boxes. The boxes were red in colour. The lid had a wild Turkish face with a mosque in the background. I was very fond of this kind. I tied my pants with a string above my ankles and stowed the boxes one by one in these extended pockets. Above the knee they were tied again and stuffed full. Above the belt, cigarette armour was again put on around the body. The brown work suit and the mackintosh covered everything nicely. Only my gait was a little strange.

So I walked the long way to the camp. My effort to keep as inconspicuous a posture as possible next to the guard must have warmed me up considerably, because when I was in my barracks afterwards and let the outer cover fall off me, I noticed that the pretty little pictures of the cigarette boxes had left big red patches on my skin. The cardboard boxes were all soaked. Such severe shingles had never been diagnosed before. All I needed now was to present myself to the doctor the following day with these strange symptoms and the usual "mis-pronunciations". I would certainly have been exchanged via Switzerland so as not to infect anyone with this strange epidemic that some twisted German wanted to introduce again.

But you could also be polished in the department stores.

There was a steel skeleton building as big as a Zeppelin hangar. That was the king of the big warehouses. The Americans called it a "hangar". Here they had to do hard labour. The mountains of flour sacks, oat sacks and wheat sacks rose before us like Egyptian pyramids. The stairs to their summits were made of the sacks themselves. One sack at a time went up "on top" as the Americans said. When you had spent 4-5 hours up these stairs with a bulging sack, you were fed up and would rather drag railway sleepers made of freshly cut fir trunks through the rain.

These two commands were the two we hated the most.

Coal trimming was no longer our business. The general prisoners had to do that. General prisoners were the American soldiers in punishment companies. The way they were treated gave them reason to envy us. Behind their fly-wire fence, grey misery dwelled in every nook and cranny. We often helped the poor guys out, no matter how careful the guards were. We did this because there were so many Germans among the general prisoners.

After the enemy allies had divided their German booty of material among themselves, we once again got to see a plethora of German guns and vehicles. They were lined up not far from us in a large square. 10 railway locomotives were also brought to us by German railwaymen. In this way we got direct news from Germany for once, but it did not differ much from the announcements in the press. The railwaymen were able to return to Germany immediately.

Now the locomotives were standing there, and the Americans were eagerly trying them out until they no longer ran. That was when the German prisoners were supposed to develop their art again. But we didn't have any prisoners who could handle the engine, at least that's what we claimed. It was too stupid for the captain that among 490 men there should be no one who could operate a railway locomotive. He therefore picked out the locksmiths from the list of occupations and renamed them railwaymen. The result was that they now took the opportunity to bring the locomotives even more into disrepair. When he complained about this and wanted to call this self-evident sabotage, he was told that railwaymen had not been in the front line. They had been used as engineers corps and locksmiths could not handle such complicated things.

If our journey home had to be managed with these machines, we would have already got the things going, but of course it didn't work like that.

American Ford boxes, on the other hand, our people could get going quite nicely, even when they already had the “passport” for the car graveyard attached to them. In return, the "car doctors" were allowed to take a little trip to the countryside after the repair.

Unfortunately, it once happened that on such a test drive through St. Sulpice a child ran into a wing and was killed. The French immediately filed a complaint, and a big kerfuffle was underway. On investigation it also emerged that the Germans had been driving without an American escort. To make the whole affair go away, the Americans paid 12,000 Frcs. compensation and let the matter die down.

Along with the cannons, rifles and machine guns, the Americans had received an enormous amount of German ammunition. A nice selection was shipped to America with the “shooting tools”, where the loot is now displayed in every town as a trophy of victory.

However, a huge amount of ammunition was also sunk into the sea. The murderous war material, however, did not want to go without song and quietly the way of all things earthly, in its death itself caused a great fish mortality in the coastal sea. The French fishermen's cooperatives, however, soon smelled a rat and knocked on the "golden" allies’ wallet by having the government file a claim for damages. Then these strange funerals stopped.

Now the Americans burned the ammunition. They did not do this themselves, however, but commissioned the prisoners to do it. On one such occasion there was a fire accident that killed German and American soldiers. As a result the prisoners were no longer available for this work. Orders and threats were of no use. The work was no longer done. So punitive measures, the "Allrights" thought. It was no use either! Then the striking company was replaced by another. But this one also refused to do the work, because it was mysteriously informed of the tragedy. The comrades had written the whole incident in telegram style under the battens of the beds. From the lower beds, the telegram could be read without difficulty.

On a Sunday afternoon the news leaked out that our company would have to provide a detachment to the ammunition depot from Monday onwards. When the orders for the following day were handed in in the evening, we found our suspicions confirmed. 50 men were to be assigned to a new, unspecified detachment. What was it? The Americans were too cowardly to tell us where they were working and wanted to present us with a fait accompli, make all sorts of fuss and take credit from headquarters for the fact that Comp. 27 under Escort 214 was doing the work that had been strictly refused on various occasions. We had smelled a rat, however, and decided to adjust accordingly. The command was provided by suitable people according to its task.

The rules of conduct were discussed in detail. We were prepared for the consequences to be expected. The next morning, I marched out to the gate with 50 men. Two lowries[26] (trucks) were waiting outside. The appearance of the captain gave the march out a special significance. There was already something like a fighting atmosphere in the air. No sooner had we covered a short distance on the Lowries than the joking started, "Where are you going, corporal?

> "To the ammunition depot" was the reply.
> "The journey is pointless" was my next announcement.
> The corporal at that; "Why?"
> "We don't work on ammunition," I told him. "That is forbidden".
> "You don't need to work to make ammunition," the corporal replied to me then. "You only have to destroy them, and that can't be forbidden, can it?

I maintained that any involvement with ammunition was forbidden by our military law and that we would not transgress this prohibition.

"If that is the view of your comrades, then we might as well go back in," the corporal now said.

---

[26] Author's original spelling

"Of course, this view is the common property of all prisoners of war," I told him firmly. "A vote will confirm this".

So it was held.

The occupants of the two cars now confirmed by raising their right arms that they would refuse to work in the ammunition depot.

"Fine, let's drive in," was the word after this oath. And we drove back to the camp. The captain was still at the gate when we returned.

"By the devil, what's the matter with you coming back," he shouted to the commanding officer.

The corporal tightly reported our refusal to work to him, which he had actually expected, otherwise he wouldn't have got up so early to supervise our marching out. But now the shouting started.

"Interpreter!"
"Sir?"
"Do you also know what you are about to do?"
"Yes, sir."
"Why don't you want to work?"
"We still want to work, but we cannot and do not want to be engaged in munitions work in any way, because our articles of war forbid us to do such work."
"Surely no articles of war can forbid you to destroy ammunition, you camel!" You

are a ringleader and will be shot! "All men are arrested".

The mood was broken. Now the captain chased the posts around. One barrack was robbed of its sleeping bags. Even the earth was dug up with spades and searched for tins of food so that we had no food apart from the water and bread provided for us.

Now two guards with mounted side arms came to each of the two exits of the barracks and finally we were allowed to enter the naked barracks. There we sat with our “cleanly washed” necks. Now we had a fight again. For once, not everything was going the usual way. No more mouthing off, now we had to whistle. The threat of shooting was nonsense, I knew that for a fact. The escort could not carry out this last resort of criminal law against us as they saw fit. A court martial had to be set up. We could still be told that it was ammunition work, which was permitted and ordered by court martial. It was no longer so easy to bump someone off. What a lot of paperwork there was when someone died. Large questionnaires, medical certificates and witness statements had to be made out in so and so many copies to headquarters. And now shots were simply going to be popped off. Out of the question. Stay calm. Let it all come together courageously.

On the second day we had the guards so far that they gave us leave to go to the kitchen. Of course, the connection with our company comrades did not break off. They supplied us with plenty of food, tobacco and cigarettes. We did not suffer any real hardship. It was just a bit boring. Every morning the captain came to us. His question as to whether we wanted to work now was always answered in the affirmative, of course with the restriction that we would not work on ammunition. But since our crime was so great that the disciplinary punishment, he was entitled to give was not sufficient; we were supposedly being charged at the court martial. I therefore eagerly waited to be questioned by a big fellow (a senior officer), but none came, and I was not taken to any. We had already been away for a week. Voices were already making themselves heard that wanted to stop the passive resistance. However, it was only a few whiners who were no longer in the mood.

They were simply replaced with other comrades. Since we were only one number, it was not difficult to replace them. On the 9th day, the captain appeared again with his troop. He was already grinning when he stood on the doorstep. After he had received his report, he told me that news had arrived from headquarters that we prisoners could only be taken for light camp work. With the ammunition disposal, which was not without danger, this was meant as a concession and was in no way meant to be a confirmation of our view. With that our detention was lifted. Our barrack was soon given back its usual appearance by handing over the sleeping bags and other equipment that had been taken out.

Illustration 7: Prisoner of War 1919

20.Camp Life

In the opinion of the American doctors, vaccination was one of the many preventive measures to maintain health. They therefore practised it quite extensively. What were we not vaccinated against? And the portions that were injected into our arms, legs or chests were not sparingly measured. Nor was it possible to squeeze past these ordeals. The Germans were less careful. There, with a little finesse, one could slurp up half a dozen vaccinations. Just as you could get past the gas mask tests in the stink room. That was not possible here.

It seemed to me to be typical of the American medical profession in general that its main focus was on avoiding disease. This spared them the difficult side of the matter, the cure.

What could excite doctors extraordinarily were the signs of epidemic diseases. Once there had been an outbreak of diphtheria among the prisoners. Now, however, assiduous efforts were made to nip the spread of this disease in the bud.

None of the 22,000 people in the whole "base" escaped close examination. Wherever we were, the doctors fell upon us and tore our mouths open. I was at the railway construction in the new harbour area, which was rising out of the flood again after a long winter rain, when the strangle commission came out to us. "Line them up" - the command rang out. And the Aesculap[27] people were already looking at the maws that had been opened with a spoon, so that one's breath was taken away. Anyone who was in any way suspicious was segregated from us and placed in a tent. In the meantime, the swab from the reddened throat was examined in the laboratory, and if the result was positive, the guy was taken to the epidemic hospital. Most of the suspects, however, only enjoyed a few days of "rest" in the cold tents and then came back to us.

This scrupulous caution on the part of the Americans and the clean and healthy way of life that we enjoyed, on the whole prevented the spread of epidemics on a large scale, as they were otherwise very likely to occur in prison camps.

Spring found us again more or less eager to build roads. However, it was now more a matter of maintaining existing roads and railways than of building new ones. On the basis of an agreement with the French, the Americans had to restore the roads and streets, which had been badly damaged by the heavy lowries or trucks and the caterpillar wheels of the guns, to their "previous condition" by 1 May.

The French road-network had been in very good order when the Americans began their activities in this area. The clean but light

---

[27] There was a car was called Aeskulap that was aimed at doctors and physicians. See https://www.pan-european-automobile-history.com/encyclopedia

connecting roads had suffered a lot from the "pressure" of traffic conditions. We therefore had plenty of work, but it did not fully satisfy the French. They could not agree to the superficial manner of the Americans and repeatedly refused to take over the roads as "healed". That the understanding between the allies thus became more and more fragile was a source of satisfaction to us. The Americans, especially the ordinary soldiers, developed more and more into allies of ours under these tensions.

One afternoon, as we were walking back from the workplace to the camp and passed a French village on the way, we got into a fight with the French because we were whistling and humming a national song. In their rage, the Frenchmen threw stones, bottles and other gifts that were worthless to us, from behind hedges and fences into our marching column. The guards, who had to watch over us so that no one could harm us, not being lazy, grabbed their heavy Colt pistols and blindly slammed into the hedges so that the *Schangels*[28] chose the better part of valour and hastily scattered. Since we were not particularly restrained on this occasion either, the rage of the French grew even greater. It gradually spread to almost all the representatives of the Grande Nation who came into contact with us. The returning French soldiers in particular had the knife sharpened on us, as the saying goes.

---

[28] See footnote 2 – Slang for the French from "Jean"

If we used the factory train to get back to the camp from work, then in the late afternoon we met the holiday train to Bordeaux. The high-spirited passengers liked to throw empty wine bottles, tin cans and other rubbish at us in addition to the "friendly words". Due to the low speed at the track junction to our camp, the holidaymakers had a nice opportunity to do this. Our guards had grown tired of this too. So they kept a sharp lookout and it happened that the "two-storey man", as we called an American who was as long as a tree, hit the windows of the wagon with his butt until there was no Frenchman's head left. "*I knock them out the nose a little of the stright*"[29] ("I'll knock their noses out of the way"), he said confident of victory. There was no more dumping that day.

The two-storeyed one knew no inhibitions in other respects either. We had to feel that bitterly on another occasion. He couldn't walk slowly, and we were so good at it. It was part of our trade. On a march to the workplace, he brought up the rear. His yelling "Hurry up!" we ostentatiously ignored. The corporal, who went ahead with me, didn't mind either but told me of his Sunday experience in Bordeaux. Suddenly we heard shouting from the rear and stopped. The angry two-storey man had gone berserk and had stabbed three men in the buttocks with his bayonet. One of the three had hit the ground and was roaring like a bull. The two-storeyed man was pale with rage when I came to him with the

---

[29] Author’s direct language

corporal. Trembling, he obeyed the corporal's order to surrender his weapons. The wounded and the two-storey man were taken to the camp.

Such rashness was very rare in our midst. It therefore raised a lot of dust and had the effect that for weeks to come the treatment regulations were handled a little more precisely and more inconveniently for us.

However, the two-storeyed one ceased to be our governess for a long time.

The suicide of our comrade Wassermann also occurred during this time. Although he had it no worse and no better than anyone else, he could not bear to wait. He became strange and finally profound. The degree of his illness could not be determined. Nevertheless, a small circle of comrades had taken it upon themselves to influence him in an appropriate way and to prevent him from doing anything stupid. However, because he did not carry out the threats of suicide that he had made several times, the concern for him eased somewhat. There was a tendency to assume that Wassermann wanted to assert himself in this way.

But oh, one foggy morning, which had had a particularly strong effect on his mind, he suddenly jumped out of the group that had stepped out of the track because of the approaching train and threw himself between the locomotive and the tender. He was crushed and disintegrated into a formless mass. I wonder if it was better as a shapeless corpse to wait for the journey home. We doubted it and felt sorry for the poor devil. The great homesickness had seized him and worn him down senseless.

Fatal accidents were not uncommon in the rampant way the Americans drove their trains around, without having provided the railway operation with an effective signalling system. However, no accident has shaken us as much as this one, which Wassermann himself wanted to happen. The locomotive driver, who believed in his own negligence, stood trembling and crying next to the pulpy corpse.

With the first signs of spring, the urge to wander grew in us, which of course could only mean escape.

Even the preparations for this enjoyed the significance of anticipation.

Who among us did not entertain such thoughts? Emigration clubs and advice centres for "foundations" were formed behind the barbed wire. The results of failed escape attempts were evaluated for new ventures. Escape contracts with or without suspensive or annulling conditions were concluded among themselves.

One such "contract", for example, had the following content: Comrade A made a binding agreement with Comrade B that they would escape on 1 May if peace had not been concluded by then and if it had not been determined when the prisoners would be extradited. Map, compass, clothes had to be ready by then. The ammunition "money" had to be procured.

There were many ways to escape. The way to the Spanish border, the Pyrenees, was not far. The Spanish workers were happy to talk to us about escape possibilities and also gave language lessons.

The most promising option was to escape under the mask of a French peasant. It was the easiest to finance because the clothes could either be made by us or stolen outside.

The escape was expediently not started from the camp, but from the workplace, which had to be located as "shady" as possible. In the 5 hours of work in the morning, a good distance could be covered before the loss was noticed during the count at noon. But when the command "a man short" was given and the count was always too low, there was a great commotion among the guards. They searched and cursed, and we made the most innocent faces and could not even explain that one should be missing.

Eventually the posts consoled themselves with the thought that the count in the morning might not have been right. It was sometimes "one man short" and eventually it turned out that some guy had joined up with another commando. But if the company was still one man short at the general count in the camp, then we had all kinds of trouble.

The Americans couldn't understand why anyone would voluntarily give up their bacon and white bread.

They were therefore very annoyed when a card suddenly arrived from Madrid, thanking them for the benefits they had received.

The most ingenious farewell was given by an interpreter from our neighbouring company, who, as an American officer in field uniform, ran way and partly covered the way to the border in a car driven by Americans. No wonder the escort took a special interest in us. It told us at times, "*I take a good care on you*". "*Dont tray to askape*" (Try not to escape).

Time and again, however, homesickness and a thirst for adventure forced this or that person to prefer the risk of escape to camp life, which was bearable in itself.

The peace dictate of May 1919 did not change our fate either.

We still had to do our work in the sweltering southern heat. The sun sucked the winter fat from our bones, stewed us like kaffirs and tore our skin to shreds. We grew thinner and thinner.

Now that peace had been concluded, we felt our retention was particularly bitter and contrary to law and morality. The Americans shared this view of ours and put us off until the treaty was ratified. Of course, we had no idea of this, which is why we were of the opinion that it was only a filibustering manoeuvre to have a semblance of legal grounds for our servitude. For us, the decisive factor was that Germany had transported the prisoners home, and the enemies had not. Anything that tried to eat up this fundamental legal concept of our question like parasites, by all sorts of surreptitious means and reinterpretations, we regarded as fraud and idiosyncratic scoundrelism. The scorching heat of the sun had left so much clear thinking in our heads. We became more and more rebellious and fought a lot with the guards, who were not really to blame for the fact. They wanted to go home themselves, in order to show what they had achieved in Europe for the achievement of world peace.

Among these guards were quite outstanding figures. It was worthwhile to make observations about them. The average American soldier, as could be seen from a closer look, was in every respect far below the average German soldier. This must be said in particular of the "drafted" soldiers, i.e. those who had not voluntarily found their way into the American army. They were a motley crew, hardly able to speak English, and represented a very strange conglomeration of people with little cultural unity. These people also did not really know for whom and for what they were fighting. They had been taught certain desirable ideas by clever propaganda, which found expression in a handbook that every soldier possessed. This was based on the deliberately erroneous assumption that Germany was a barbarian state which was well on the way to subordinating and raping the whole world if it was not opposed with all possible means. With a great deal of effort, the authors of this handbook had invented all the horrors that were likely to turn the superficially thinking American masses of people against us "Huns".

I often took the trouble to go through this important booklet sentence by sentence with Americans whose mentality allowed it and to refute it with my arguments. Given the American's inherent obtuseness, my preaching was not always immediately successful. I also lacked the necessary vocabulary for such unusual phrases. Nevertheless, the Americans could not ignore my views on these matters.

I once had a heated argument with a corporal because he claimed that one of his cousins, an Englishman, had been wounded and taken prisoner by the Germans and had been treated horribly in the military hospital. Among others, a German nurse had loosened the hub from the wheel of the operating trolley in the military hospital so that he would fall off the trolley on the way to the operating theatre, because the removal of the hub meant that the wheel had to come loose when the trolley was used. I was so outraged at this fistful of lies that this fellow heretically threw into our debate that I threw hearty rudeness at his head, which led to a scuffle. It was only with great difficulty that we brawlers could be separated.

I could no longer get along with this mouthy fellow.

Of course, the lad wanted to get back at me one day when we were working on the woodpile. There we had to carry railway sleepers.

We did it in such a way that one man took the sleeper on his shoulder and the end of the sleeper was carried on a stick by two men. These sleeper transports looked like mass funerals. We always muttered "rhubarb, rhubarb, rhubarb" so that the work would not become too monotonous.

The hostile corporal took the work as a game and forbade the mumble. But when we noticed that he was annoyed by it, we did it all the more. Only we made sure that he couldn't tell exactly which porters were muttering. We enjoyed that immensely.

Now he wanted the railway sleepers to be carried by two men. We refused and said that, firstly, it was too heavy, that we had always carried the sleepers like this for four years during the war and we kept it that way, and secondly, that the work process was none of his business. He should make sure that no one escaped. We would already move our quantum of sleepers.

The dispute was finally settled by the engineer to the effect that we should carry the heavy timbers on with 3 men without murmuring. So, he was neither right nor wrong, and that makes one happy. It is clear that the corporal soon took other opportunities to drag us along somehow.

But the wooden troop was put together in such a way that the corporal's efforts in this respect bounced off our unity, which finally persuaded him to calm down again and behave in an orderly manner.

We also had our difficulties with an *ingeneer*[30] on the railway, whom we called Heini. His name was also Henry. He was a stubborn, moody hussy who nobody could please. Once he was put together with an "education squad" that "worked" him to the bone.

For such slave owners, who disturbed the common good, we always had an education squad ready, who were happy to do their job for the oppressed comrades.

Remarkable types belonged to this strike force of practical achievement. For example, there was the long Becker from Colonia, a plasterer by trade. He was the strongest man in the company, if weightlifting is to be taken as a measure of his strength. No one could beat him. Unfortunately, his strength was not matched by his beauty, which was a great annoyance to him. His facial features also lacked beauty and regularity. This rough core, however, concealed a good-natured heart. The long Becker was always ready to help. We therefore liked him very much. Unfortunately, the Becker was not satisfied with being the strongest prisoner; he also wanted to be the most beautiful. He would not have stood up to a beauty contest. He therefore relied on his strength and wrestled down anyone who did not want to acknowledge him as the most beautiful prisoner. When he had laboriously overcome all opposition in this way, he had a certificate issued to him in the clerk's office that he was the most

[30] Author's spelling (engineer)

beautiful. With his strength and goodness, he was the soul of the education strike force. He also chose his companions according to the educational task he was given. Never did he fail. The little Saxon Richard was never missing from his company. I have not remembered his family name. No one knew him by his real name.

Richard was as fat as he was tall. In winter he was even fatter. He had such nice piggy eyes, which were completely covered by his chubby cheeks, especially when he put on his service face. Once, as usual on Sunday morning, we were dressed spick and span in the camp for roll call, the captain stopped just in front of Richard as he passed, looked at the little, fat "plug" and said, "He won't see home again. When Richard looked up in fright at the captain, who was also as fat as he was, but much bigger, the captain added with a laugh: "His eyes are growing shut". That was the end of the critical situation for Richard. Nevertheless, he was uncomfortable on the following Sundays when he heard the top sergeant's call: "Line them up, ten o'clock, full dress".

He thought the last two words of the Top were bad German and therefore corrected them to his liking. This characterised Richard's mood and his preference for the captain's "inspections". As a bright Saxon, Richard usually did not owe an answer to anyone. Only when he was asked for the 1,000,000th time, "Richard, what is “eier[31] Genich” doing?" did he remain silent. Without Richard, imprisonment would not have been bearable. That is certain.

Another fighter in the circle of the "Becker people" was Max from Berlin. He had an indefinable face. His chunky head seemed to have been hewn out of a block of wood with an axe. One always had the impression that the face was not quite finished being modelled. Maxe was distinguished by the well-known monosyllabicity of the Berliners. What the whole gang thought up slowly and laboriously, Maxe said "calmly" in one fell swoop. His muzzle went like a machine gun. Maxe was Becker's advocate. When Max eyed the situation with his melancholy gaze under bushy eyebrows, he had grasped everything worth knowing in one moment. The "beautiful" Becker could not follow his Berlin speech fast enough, as if shot from a pistol. The discussion, which had to lead to a complete grasp of the day's affairs, took place in the evening in a corner of the barracks.

One of Becker's faithful was the farmer Schwammborn from the Bergisches Land. Wherever he hit with his heavy paw, no grass grew any more. Schwammborn was not a heavy farmer. This may be said of his physical movement as well as his mental agility. His physique did not show the strength that was

---

[31] “Eier” = eggs but phonetically close to “euer” meaning “your”. “Genich” phonetically close to “Koenig” being king.

inherent in him. However, he used it sparingly, as he generally weighed everything on a gold scale, so to speak. Becker didn't like to miss him either. Today he is in America. Hopefully, his dealings with the bear drivers, as he called the Americans, have been beneficial to his development in the U.S.A.

Since I cannot sketch all the representatives of the Education Club, I will end with Cream Slice, a lanky confectioner. Although I mention him last, he is not inferior in rank to his comrades described above. The cream slice's real name was Schulz, he was still young and came from Iserlohn. His head bobbed on his long, narrow neck like a springy hazelnut whip. With his cheeky ascension nose in a milky face that was actually only a hint of a face, he sniffed around everywhere and always smelled the roast first. His bubbling mind was inexhaustible in clever ideas and fidgety jokes. At times, he trusted his weak body construction too much to match that of his stronger comrades.

Unimaginable is the variety with which a group that had the characteristics described above waged war with a miserable tormentor of peaceful prisoners at the plagued workplace. If such a guy could not be brought down with the one method, then they resourcefully resorted to another. After all, the carrion of an American was just as much in the wool as a Prussian sergeant in the barracks yard who had set himself the task of taking down a hardened old man in re-exercise.

Illustration 8:Peter and Cream Slice

21.More Waiting

As the American soldiers' prospect of returning home grew, so did their addiction to war memorabilia. Almost pathological was their greed for objects that were even remotely likely to represent a connection with the World War. It was not possible to honestly satisfy the Americans' wishes in this respect. It was necessary to resort to creations. The imagination gave us a wide scope and an almost unlimited field of activity with regard to these fashion creations. The souvenir workshops behind barbed wire developed from the most modest beginnings with the most primitive means into true art workshops.

This industriousness in the creation of souvenirs of all kinds was not developed because of the beautiful eyes of the Americans. Nor were they given to them as gifts of love across the pond, no, a financial exploitation of the childish simplicity of the bear drivers developed. The beautiful products had to be paid for and were sometimes highly priced. Trade and change flourished with all its bright and dark sides. It was always a royal merchant who traded. The coloured soldiers in particular were taken for a ride. But how those crazy pikes were also after everything that shone. If our artists had spent the whole of Sunday diligently trying to make series of "wedding rings" out of a brass tube, then on Monday morning one could make the observation that the trading agents wore a beautifully polished ring on their finger and had a lot of scratching about in their faces, until at last the savages eagerly besieged the owner and made offers on the beautiful golden ring. The more the ring owner rebelled against selling it, the more these stupid bitches offered for the ring. The most fantastic prices were made in this way from such worthless trinkets. Once the Negroes had the beautiful rings on their greasy, mischievous claws for a day, then the shine was gone, and the buyer was also teased by his fellow Negroes. Of course, he never found the cunning seller to whom he had sworn bloody revenge. The lesson that not all that glitters is gold had, after all, cost the black man his 20 Frcs.

The most beautiful signet rings were made from cookware aluminium and combs. Particularly attractive items were the flower vases artfully made from cartridges. But these were also splendid pieces. I enjoyed following the working process. The cartridges, after an iron tube had been inserted and molten lead poured between the tube and the brass wall, were worked with hammer and steel. The rim was beaten out on an anvil in beautiful lines. Now it was greased and polished to such an extent that it had a way. Finally, the souvenir of the world was complete. Of course, such a splendid specimen brought in a nice amount of money. 10 - 20 dollars were paid for these pieces and, measured against the sold of the Americans and in view of the work done, that was really not too much. However, only very few comrades took on such specialised work. Painters and draughtsmen sold their varied products at low prices. The initially good prices were soon too much lowered by the growing supply.

The American dentists were even interested in our dentures. Unfortunately, they did so on a Sunday afternoon. We were just about to take our siesta when the gate was ripped open, and a medical van came rushing in. What does that mean, we said to ourselves? The cinema truck in the middle of the afternoon? Have the Americans gone crazy? A similar car had already been with us late in the evening. It contained the reproduction machine and other utensils for the moving-pictures (cinema). The cinema operators had hurriedly attached a large white cloth to bamboo poles and stretched it out, folded down the front and rear walls of the power wagon and we had a cinema performance in our camp yard. Even if we were not presented with any brilliant performances, we were grateful for the attention. It was not to be expected that the Americans would give us an afternoon show, they were not ready yet, even though they came from the land of unlimited possibilities. A certain degree of darkness is part of a cinema performance. So there had to be another reason for the car.

We were soon taught about this. Two Red Cross people crept from the car. They dragged buckets and boxes into the exhibition hall and then even two operating chairs. The Red Cross people were the executioners of the dentists and nurses who appeared in another van. Now we were all presented to the doctors who looked at our dentures and tapped on our teeth. Teeth that were not healthy were pulled out without anaesthetic, even if there were 10 or 12 of them in one mouth. That was quick. We were to get replacements later. Judging by the many gold-shining American snouts, the doctors could make us beautiful dentures if they wanted to. If they had approached the renewal as spiritedly as they did the ripping out, we would have been fine out of it. But the guys left us in the lurch and never came back to us. They left more than 200 victims on the bloody field of tooth slaughter on a Sunday afternoon. Howling and gnashing their teeth (as far as their remaining chewing tools still allowed), the "treated" sat bent over their horse buckets in front of the mess hall, spewing blood and bile. The whole beautiful afternoon was ours for the taking. Even the evening meal had to be changed to 1st food (slime soup). The worst cinema would have been nicer. The things one didn't have to put up with as a prisoner. We decided that in the next war we would have to take care of American prisoners on the side. As far as we were concerned, they should have it no better and no worse than we had it with them now.

After we had repaired the road network to our satisfaction and the Americans began to sell their immense stocks of goods to their friendly states and small towns "on nick", we were busy again in the warehouses. Whether France, Poland, Rumania, Lithuania, Latvia, Estonia, Czechoslovakia, everyone was scrambling around big rich brother America and trying to steal what was not nailed down. Since the goods were of course only loaded and transported under military cover, we got to know the soldiers of all these partly new towns. We always knew how to take excellent revenge for the particularly friendly treatment we received. We even went to the trouble of opening large 1 cbm. wooden boxes and sorting the shoes. We were happy to do this voluntary work because it meant that the boxes for Poland, for example, contained only right shoes and the boxes for Romania only left shoes. We didn't care if the puffed-up wretches had to pick their shoes up and down the country or put their legs in a different way. And if the French annoyed us, they got flour that had gone sticky in leaky barracks. The Intendantur[32] officials were then annoyed to no end.

When counting the sacks and boxes, the Americans, who always hanged their work pretty high so that they couldn't get at it so easily, relied entirely on us. What our stopwatch showed, had entered the railway wagon. The storekeepers inevitably certified that on the delivery note and charged for it too. I had always heard so much about double-entry American bookkeeping. I even struggled once in a course to book fictitious business transactions according to the rules of this accounting. Here in the big American business with a turnover of millions, however, I had the perception that in practice the Americans did not care at all about the legality of this accounting. I have not yet come across such a

---

[32] Term used in Prussia for temporary employees paid out of budget whose service could be terminated immediately.

straightforwardness in management as was in practice with the storekeepers. Between each of the two warehouses there was a small, inconspicuous wooden house in which lived an enormous man, the storekeeper of the two mammoth barracks. In his little house was the American commercial management, which was limited to collecting delivery notes on incoming and outgoing goods on a newspaper hook. The difference between the quantities on the delivery slips on the two newspaper hooks represented the stock. The storekeeper had to certify its accuracy. He did so without hesitation, because it was not possible to determine the stock and it was never done. A circumstance that the storekeepers exploited to their own advantage. The French civilian population always had a considerable need, especially for sugar, and the storekeepers for dice money. Thus, the business development of the silent partners was a given.

I have always silently wondered why none of us attempted to get locked into a railway carriage for a trip to Koblenz. It was well looked after by the Americans, but feasible such an intention would have been. Because the slogans of our return home were becoming more and more dense and could not be doubted, apparently no one wanted to risk such an illicit journey anymore.

22.The Last Wait

When we came back from work to the camp at noon on 1 August, we saw a truck with bales of straw in our yard. Ouch, cheek! So, we were to get a new filling for our straw sacks. In the whole time we had been imprisoned, straw had been given to be changed once, because the first load had turned to powder. That was five months ago. Measured against this period of time, we could still wait a long time for our journey home. It was therefore understandable that we were annoyed by the straw delivery. Cursed and stitched up, we were upset. The guards could hardly calm us down. They finally lied to us that our journey home would be on bulging straw sacks, and very soon. We actually had another 3 months to "wear out" the new straw.

In September, the Americans handed over the rest of their possessions to the French. At the same time, our activities ceased. The rest did us good for a few days. Then we got bored with camp life. The Americans knew, however, that idleness and laziness are not good in the long run. So, every morning they took us out for a long walk in the surrounding area. Like spa guests, we lay in the Gironde and sunbathed. Around noon, we arrived back at the camp with a terrible appetite. After a short rest, we had to go back to sports and games. Unfortunately, swimming, which many comrades longed to do, was denied us. In any case, too many canal swimmers were suspected among us. Competitions with other companies now developed. We even approached the escort company. To our chagrin, the Americans played poor football and didn't bother with the rules of the game. So, all the fuss was more brawl than sport.

From our walks we brought back boards to make our "reserve cases". From what were initially very primitive boxes, we gradually created pleasing, beautifully painted "souvenir boxes" with all the trimmings. Soon everyone had put together such a beautiful box. The contents swelled and swelled, and some had to build another or a larger box to accommodate all the stuff they had saved up for the journey home. But these reserve suitcases did not escape the captain's gaze. It was impossible to hide them all. So one day he asked us what strange boxes were standing around and what they contained. We told him that the contents were the "reception" that our comrades had saved up for themselves, so to speak, and then goods that had been bought in our canteen. Naturally, the captain wanted to take a look inside such a box. The box he was shown was harmless. It contained tins of cocoa or pepper, tins and sachets of tobacco, soap, chocolate drops, chewing tobacco, chewing gum and similar things. It also contained other, not so harmless things; but you couldn't see them because the box had two bottoms. I was not able to find out what was between the two bottoms. That will always remain a secret. In any case, the captain did not object to our collecting zeal.

Unfortunately, we didn't have too many more opportunities to collect, because we didn't have a field to work in. We would have liked to work in the barracks again for a week, even though they had changed hands and the French were certainly more careful than the Americans. But only rarely was a small troop lent to the Frenchmen for work duty. At the end of September, we had to go out again for several days to build roads. Here and there, there was still some beautification work to be done. In this way we came to many small towns and villages. We brought the beautiful red sand for the road surface from far away by lorry. The civilians were keen on this beautiful sand. They could use it as a surface for their garden paths. But we were careful that they didn't steal it. Sometimes, when we refused to take it away, they said we had nothing to say, but we taught them that. If they got something, then they had to pay well with wine. On one day we had drunk so much red wine that by noon we were all foggy. In order not to attract the attention of the American officers who might be coming along the way, we lay down by a cool little stream in the deep valley, took off our shoes and stockings and refreshed ourselves in the clear, cold water. The posts were, of course, even more befuddled than we were. The food truck had not found us and when it was time to leave, we took our posts under our arms and dragged them with great difficulty onto the truck that brought us home. But our vehicle driver was also in tears and drove with us on a sloping road against a closed railway barrier so that the barrier bent out of the seat, and we were halfway on the track. Thank God the train was not yet coming. Therefore, we were spared a bad outcome to this wine-filled ride. However, the fright had quickly chased away the wine mood. Finally, we arrived safely at our camp with our dented motor vehicle.

PART 5: HOME

23.Home Sweet Home

"Home, sweet home, there is no place like home" were his last words. Our pieces were loaded onto trucks and taken to the train station.

With groups swinging right march! Towards the station we went out the gate. The Americans, who saw us on the way to the station, called out their farewell greetings to us. We were quite exuberant on our last march. The captain had been promised that we would be on our best behaviour for the last few days, so that we would not drop another drop of vermouth into our cup of joy. Afterwards, however, the bottle of vermouth remained in St. Sulpice despite our many follies, and finally our reserve train, consisting of large American railway wagons, set off. It had become evening in the meantime. During the night our train made slow progress. The next day's journey was a Sunday bright and clear. It was a different journey from the previous year, when we were transported to Tours and Bordeaux and were quietly and sullenly crammed into the small cattle cars like herrings, and the great uncertainty about our distant fate ate at our despondent hearts. We now looked at the country for Frenchmen with completely different eyes. If our train touched villages and towns, then we had to hold back a little with singing and noise, so that there would be no clashes with the victory-drunk population. On the other hand, we could do whatever we wanted on the open track. We arrived in Iss-sur-Tille in the evening. At the same moment, a train left for Germany. We had the opportunity to ask our departing comrades about the conditions in Iss-sur-Tille and learned that everything went smoothly. The things we took with us were not checked very strictly. The goods that were currently "brought into captivity" would be reimbursed in pennies and nickels. This had not always been the case in the exchange camp.

In Iss-sur-Tille, Americans even gave the things to the prisoners. Apparently, they could get along better with the French than we could. We called the French guards only Froks - frogs. We got that from the Americans; they never said anything else.

When we had to stop for a long time at a small station outside Metz, we asked the Americans for permission to decorate our wagons with acacia branches. There was a small avenue of acacia trees that ran along a moat on the other side of the Lilliput station. The Americans were immediately keen on this idea and helped us to strip the few trees of their branches in a short time. The poor Frenchman who had the station "under him" grumbled and clamoured in vain. Our train resembled a moving forest when it left. Later we pulled strips of paper through the branches. The people of Metz greeted us with a warmth we had not expected. They waved and shouted incessantly. Handkerchiefs were too small for them to work with. Towels, tablecloths, even bed sheets fluttered out of the windows. At the next stop, I managed to post a telegram to my bride. Towards evening we arrived in Trier. The platform was surrounded by French colonial troops. They stood there with their side arms raised. A rather strange guard of honour for us. The Americans took great pains to avoid clashes, which could easily occur given our mood. In Trier we were fed for the first time on German soil. Then we went on to Koblenz, where we arrived in the middle of the night. Our luggage was loaded onto trolleys and in step we marched through the streets of Koblenz to the magazine. We had been forbidden to sing at the midnight hour. But the same footfall woke our compatriots even without singing. In an instant, all the windows were lit up and torn open, and a hurricane of cheers rang out. The Americans were powerless against this. Who knows whether such a spontaneous reception was given to you later in America. That same night, a German major in civilian clothes greeted us in the magazine and brought us greetings from home.

Tracked down by my telegram, my bride came over from Neuwied the very next day. It was not easy to find the right Schmitz among the many Schmitzes. And when the right Schmitz was found, the bride could not come to him because the Americans were manning the gate. So I quickly got married and introduced my wife to the top sergeant at the gate guard. My wife was allowed to visit me, of course. So, we saw each other again after almost two years of separation in a somewhat strange environment. My bride had brought her friend with her. We didn't want to put her through the long wait on the street. So,

I tried to bring her in as well. But I met with resistance, because the top knew me and would not allow me a second woman. First, hand over the other woman, he said, then you'll get a new one.

In the so-called quarantine camp on the extensive warehouse grounds, bordered on three sides by roads and surrounded by a high iron fence, we still had to fulfil a waiting period of several days. As was our custom, we were still sealed off from the environment. American guards still protected us here. Patrols tripped on the pavement of the adjoining streets, and then quickly and unexpectedly a profoundly shattering event burst into our last silent wait. A comrade threw himself out of the 4th floor window in a state of mental derangement and crashed on the pavement of the courtyard. Once more blood, once more a sad farewell. The ambulance was not yet at the gate when the twitching body was also still and dead.

"The Last Cross".

Geographic Overview

Wimar Schmitz often refers to his journey through the First World War by the names of villages and towns. He was first on the Western Front in France, then for nearly 2 and 1/2 years in the East [Lithuania, Latvia and Estonia] and again in France.

The map gives an overview:

Illustration 9: Map – Battle Fronts

The table lists all the names mentioned in the book:

Illustration 10: Table – Places and Timeline

Year	Month	Place	Activity
1914	Aug	Neuwied	[Birth place] **War & Registration**
		Bonn	[Residence]
		Rohleder, Holzlar, Niederpleis, Honnef,Koeningswinter, Venusberg	[Exercises]
		Godesberg, Mehlem, Gerolstein, Trier, Metz, Diedenhofen	Trip to the Western front
		Longwy, Sedan, Charlarange, Sommepy	First French town, Front
		St Marie e Py	Training; 2 months occupation
	Dec	**Souvain, Perthes**, / Vouziers, Rethel	Combat zone / military hospital
1915	Jan - June	Diedenhoffen, Ludwigshafen	Wounded homewards
		Mannheim	3 months healing
		Bonn	
		Kalscheuren, Luettich, Roullers, Zarren	Cow transport to Belgium front
		Brugge, Ostende, Gent, Mecheln, Antwerpen, Brussel	Short tour after cows delivery
		Landsberg and der Warthe, Tilsit (Sovesk, Kalingrad), Tauroggen (Taurgae, Lithuania)	Tri to the Eastern front
		Gouvernement Suwalki, Nowopol, Poikny, Wysocki-Dwor, Bokrischowa	Marching and fighting
	Aug - Dec	Janischki, Swienta River	Marching and fighting
		Kowarsk	Command post
		Doginze (Gara - Swienta confluence), Leljuny, Anatlogi, Uziany, Dusjaty, Schunelki	Marching battles to Dünaburg [now Daugavpils, Latvia]
		Castle Mukule, Imbrodi, Smelina [Smelinka, Lithuania], Medum & Kriwoi-Most Areas	
		Polischki, Sehktschawa [No Information can be found] near Dünaburg [now Daugavpils, Latvia]	

Year	Month	Place	Activity
1916			
			2 Year Position
1917			
		Matweikischki	
	Aug	Josephowo, Abeli, Raziwilischki, üxküll	Advance to Riga
		Riga	Day visit
	Sep	Dauzerons, Jakobstadt [Jekabpils, Latvia]	Battle for Jakobstadt
	Nov	Mitau [Jelgava, Latvia]	Temporary halt
	Dec		

Year	Month	Place	Activity
1918	Feb	Bonn	Home visit
	Mar	Riga, Vollmar, Wenden [Cēsis, Latvia], Walk [Valga], Schloss Karlsberg	Advance to Dorpat [Tartu, Estland]
		Dorpat	Occupation & Administration
	July	Riga,	West front - Flirey
	Aug	Germany, Thiacourt	Route to western front
		Flirey, Bouilonville	Battles
	Sep	Flirey	**Captivity**
		Paris - Orleans - Tours; Bordeaux; St. Sulplice	
	Nov		**Ceasefire**
1919		La Basines, Rotspon	**Prisoner of War**
	May		**Peace Dictate**
	Sep	Iss-sur-Till, Metz, Trier, Koblenz	**Home Sweet Home**

There are village and town names in "Russia" [Poland, Lithuania, Latvia and Estonia] that appear in the book and therefore the table that cannot be found directly on a map search (or Google).

For the reader who is interested, the places can be found with the help of the web resource http://easteurotopo.org/indices/kdwr/alphabetical/.

In the following maps there is an overview of the estimated distances and routes travelled by the author.

Illustration 11: Journeys of the Western Front

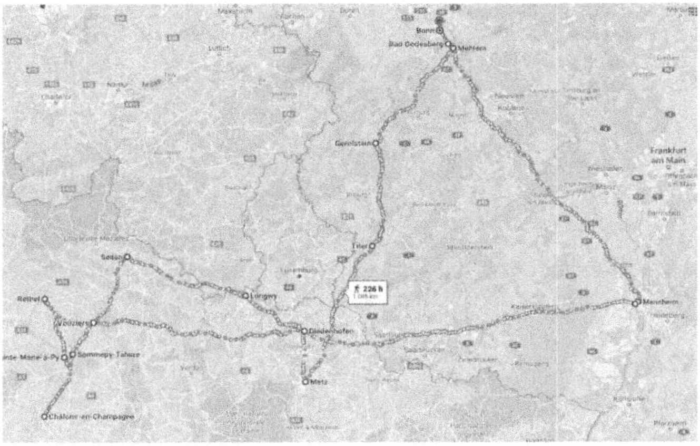

Illustration 12: Cow Transport Trip

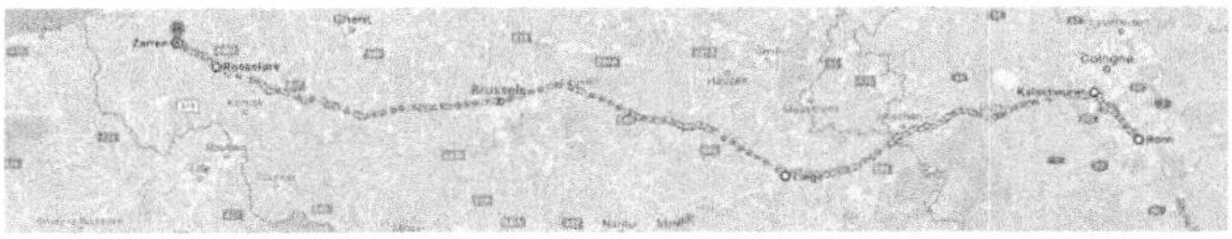

Illustration 13: "Holiday detour" after the cows delivery

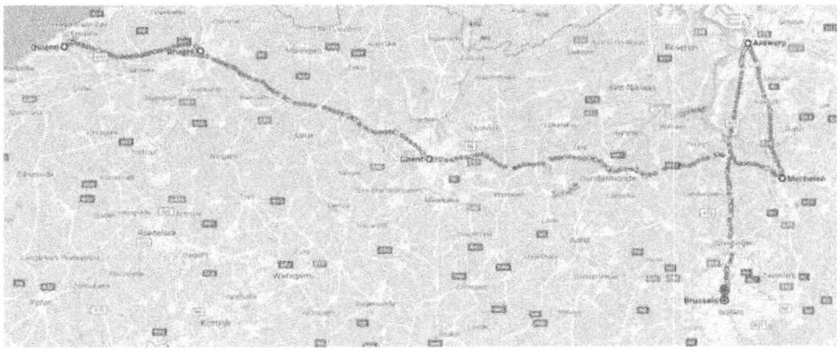

Illustration 14: East Front Journey

Illustration 15: Eastern Front Marching Battles

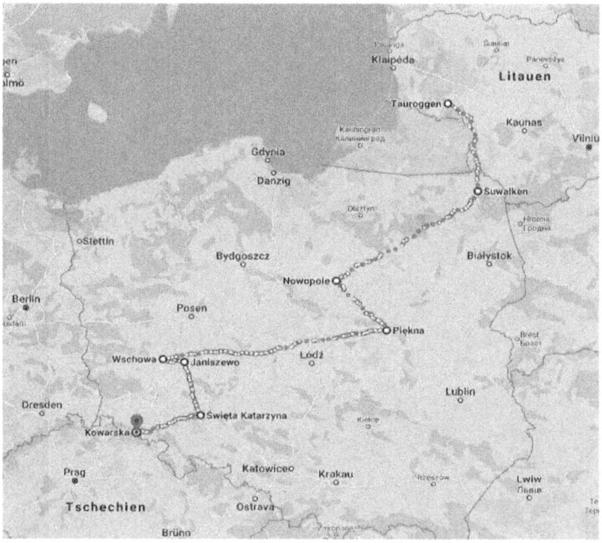

Illustration 16: March on Dünaburg (Daugavpils)

Illustration 17: March on Riga

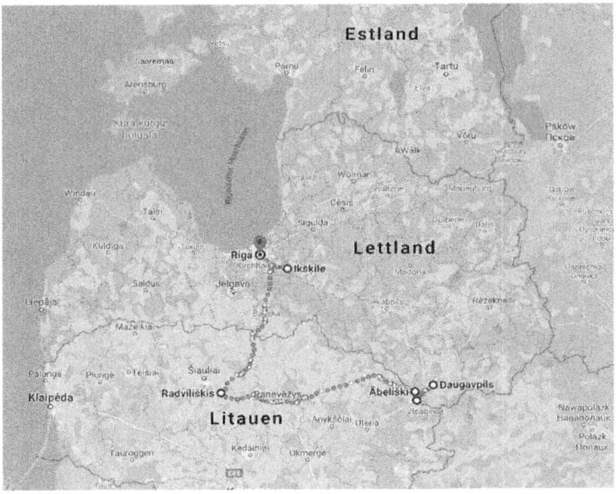

Illustration 18: Battle for Jakobstadt

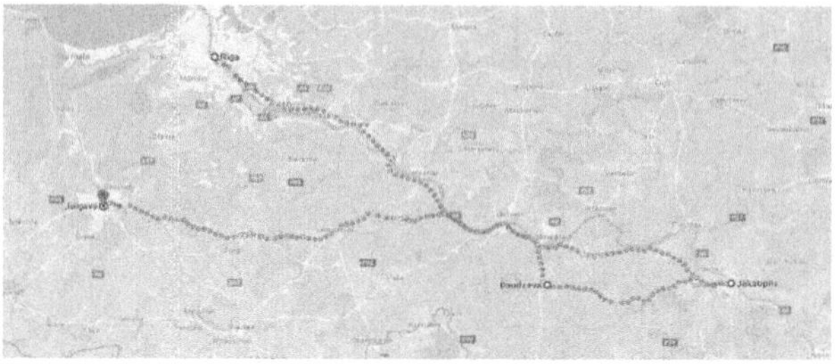

Illustration 19: March on Torpat (Tartu)

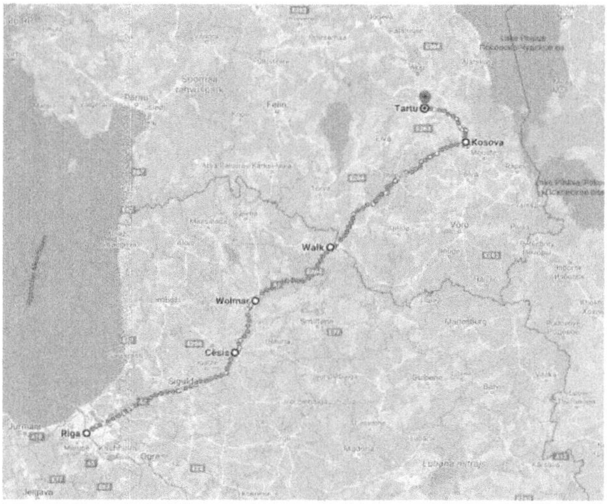

Illustration 20: 2nd Western Front & Captivity

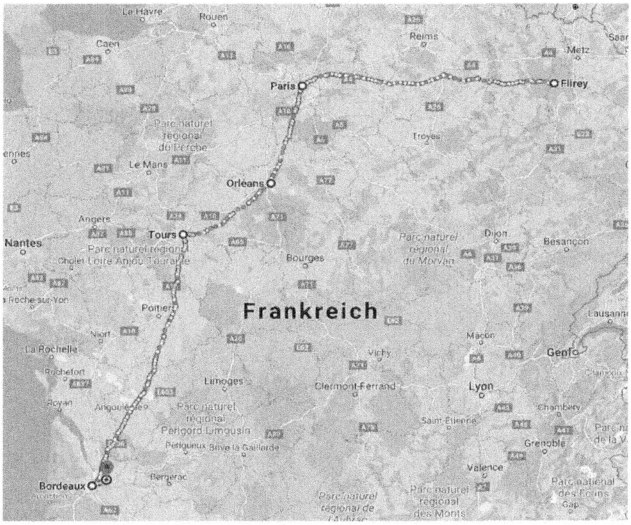

Illustration 21: Journey Home Sweet Home

Time Overview

Illustration 22: 1914 Overview

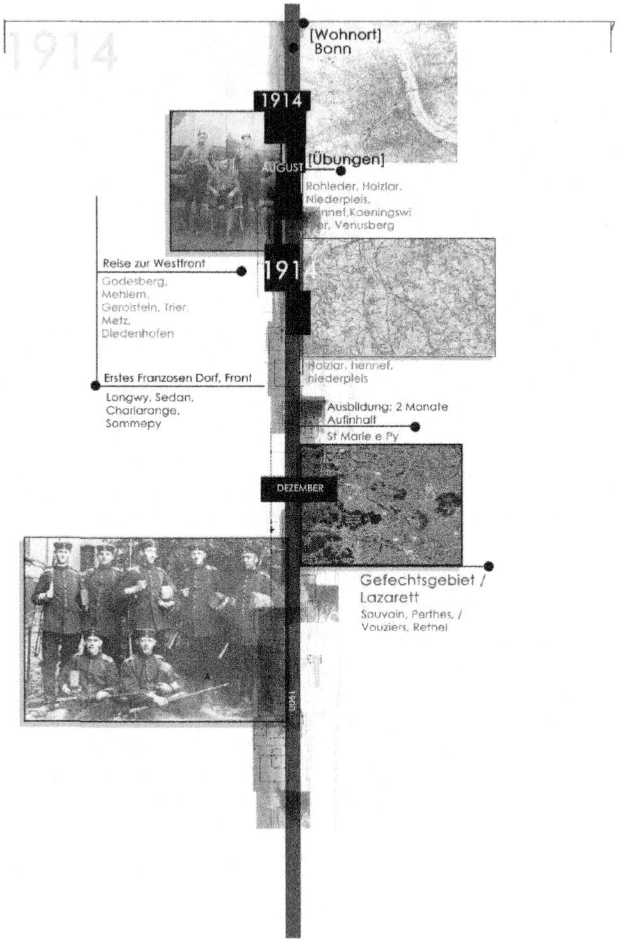

Illustration 23: 1915 Overview

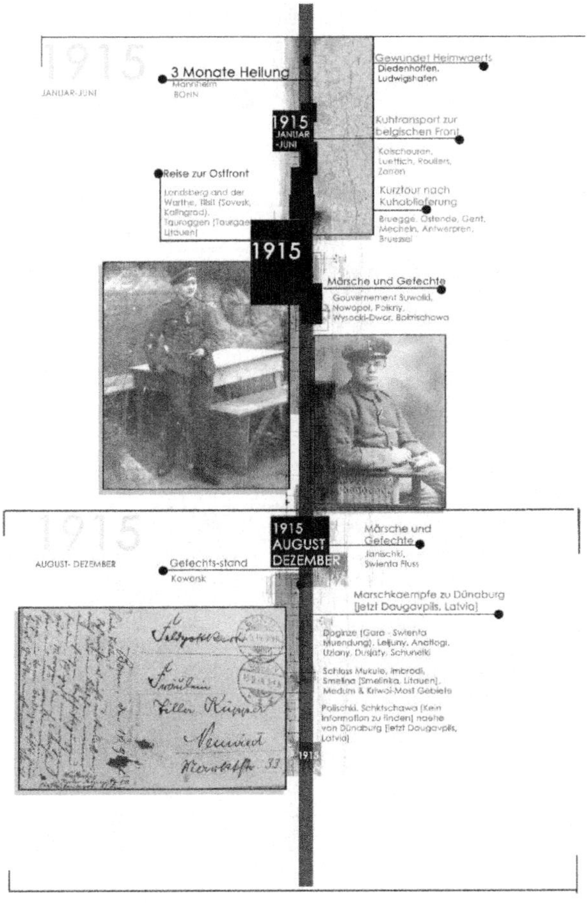

Illustration 24: 1917 Overview

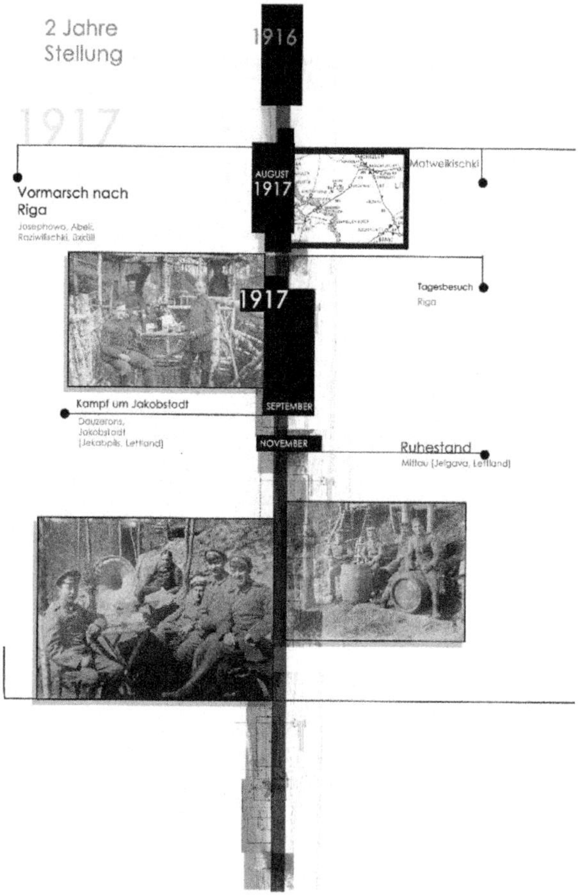

Illustration 25: 1918 & 1919 Overview

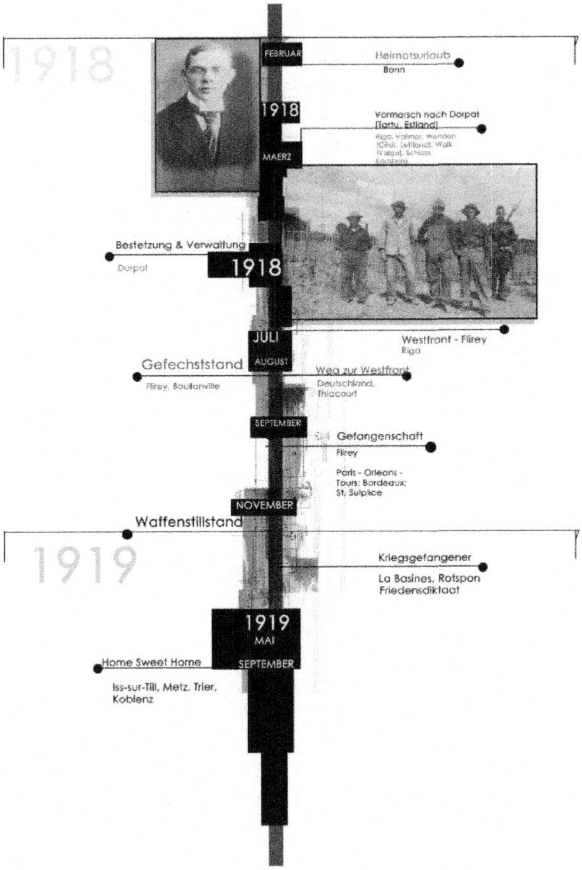

Wimar Peter Schmitz

We only knew him as the deceased grandfather / father of our mother, Anneli Jarm (gb. Schmitz) [mother-in-law of the editor].

According to the manuscript, there were 4 brothers and a sister. The author's father had already died before the war and the mother during the course of the war. The manuscript also mentions that one brother was killed in the war, one was also a prisoner of war, one was still in the war, and one was seriously wounded at home.

A surviving identity card offers little information:

Illustration 26: Identity Card Wimar Peter Schmitz

Wimar Schmitz lived for 47 years. He died in May 1938. We could not clearly determine the cause of death. Unfortunately, Wimar Schmitz's children have also been deceased for many years. Suggestions were that it may have been suicide. Whether this is true or why will forever remain a mystery. His son Günter mentioned that his father had gas gangrene.

The official death book does not mention anything either:

Illustration 27: Death Certificate Wimar Peter Schmitz

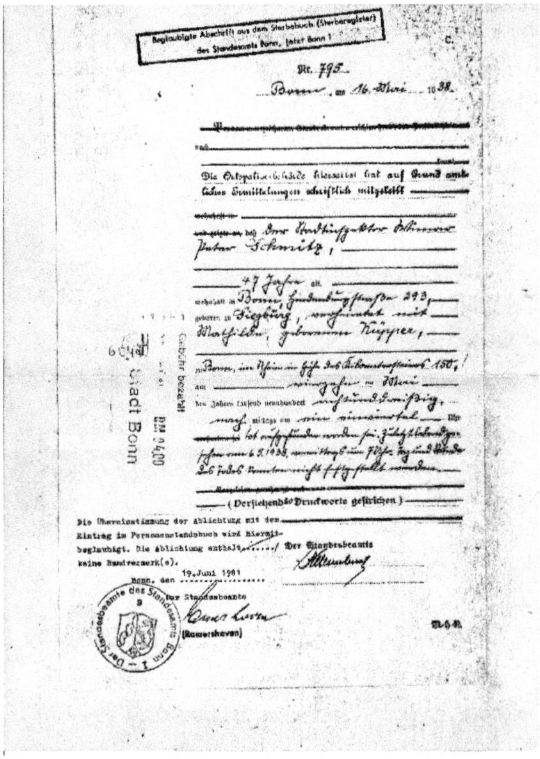

Beglaubigte Abschrift aus dem Sterbebuch (Sterberegister) des Standesamts Bonn, jetzt Bonn 1

C.

Nr. 795

Bonn, am 16. Mai 1938.

Die Ortspolizeibehörde hierselbst hat auf Grund amtlicher Ermittelungen schriftlich mitgeteilt

daß ... Wimar Peter Schmitz,

47 Jahre alt,

wohnhaft in Bonn, Hindenburgstraße 293,

geboren in Siegburg, verheiratet mit Mathilde, geborene Küpper,

in Bonn, im Rhein ... 150,

am ... Mai

des Jahres tausend neunhundert achtunddreißig,

... mittags um ... Uhr

... 6.5.1938 ...

(Vorstehend ... Druckworte gestrichen)

Die Übereinstimmung der Ablichtung mit dem Eintrag im Personenstandsbuch wird hiermit beglaubigt. Die Ablichtung enthält keine Randvermerk(e).

Der Standesbeamte

Bonn, den 19. Juni 1981

Der Standesbeamte

(Romershoven)

Der Standesbeamte des Standesamts Bonn 1

Gebühr bezahlt

Stadt Bonn

No. 795

Bonn, 16 May 1938.

The local police authority here has informed us in writing, on the basis of official investigations, that

Municipal Inspector Wimar
Peter Schmitz,
47 years old

resident in Bonn, Hindenburgstrasse 293
born in Siegburg, married to
Mathilde, née Küpper,
in Bonn, was found dead in the Rhine at kilometre stone 150,
on the fourteenth of May
of the year one thousand nine hundred and thirty-eight,
after noon at one quarter past one.
Last seen
on 6.5.1938 in the morning at 7 o'clock. The day and hour
of death could not be established.

He was married to Mathilde Schmitz [Küpper] born 7.10.1894 [Neuwied] and died 20.11.1967. They had three children:

1. Anneli Mathilda Veronika Jarm [Schmitz] born 24.02.1922 [Bonn]; died: 4.08.2000.
2. Hedwig Maria Margareta Schmitz born 19.09.1924 [Bonn] died 3.08.1999; and
3. Günter Karl Maria Schmitz born 24.12.1930 [Bonn] died 28.11.1986

Illustration 28: Family photo: Author with wife & children

A solitary family photo shows (left) Wife, Oma Küpper, Hedwig, Günter (front), Author and Anneli.

Both Anneli and Günter emigrated to South Africa and spent their lives there.

Anneli Jarm [Schmitz] had 5 children, Hendryk Kruse (father Kruse, first husband), Michiline, Christiane, Oliver and Anneli Jarm. Michiline died in 1999 but the other 4 children still live in South Africa.

Hedwig Schmitz never married.

Günter Schmitz married Elke Henke and they had two sons, Peter and Mathias. All three are still living in South Africa.

Acknowledgments

Thanks are to be given to my wife Nanu (Christiane) and:

The daughter Hedwig who kept the manuscript safe until her death.

Anneli Striebeck (Jarm) and her husband Wolfgang Striebeck, who dissolved the Hedwig household and took the manuscript, together with a few photos, to South Africa.

Anneli Jarm (Schmitz) who kept the manuscript and photos until her death.

My children, Veronika and Tilo Els who put the pressure on me to capture the manuscript electronically and publish it as a book. Veronika retyped the first pages herself in MS Word in 2018. Tilo and his fiancée (now wife) Kate Spencer (both resident in Germany since September 2020) edited the geographical maps and the time overviews, and Kate designed and drew the book cover herself.

Elke Schmitz (Henke) for the documents on Wimar Schmitz. Prof. Eberhard Funcke for the translation of the letter written in Sütterlin script.

The pages of the manuscript were photographed and electronically fixed. With thanks to the free programme "Text Fairy".

This English translation was primarily done whit the free program version of DeepL.

Printed in Great Britain
by Amazon

32551396R00145